BARRON'S SIMPLIFIED APPROACH

TO SHAKESPEARE'S

Richard II

By Bernard Grebanier
PROFESSOR EMERITUS
BROOKLYN COLLEGE

BARRON'S EDUCATIONAL SERIES, INC.
WOODBURY, NEW YORK

CONTENTS

The Date and the Sources
of *Richard II*

"*The Tragedye of King Richard the Second.* As it hath beene publikely acted by the right Honourable the Lorde Chamberlaine his Servants. London Printed by Valentine Simmes for Andrew Wise, and are to be sold at his shop in Paules church yard at the signe of the Angel. 1597." So reads the title-page of the first quarto edition of our play. Andrew Wise entered it for publication in the Stationers' Register on August 29 of that year. There are copies of this quarto extant which are corrected, others which are not.

The next year, 1598, saw the publication of a second quarto; its title-page bore the additional information: "By William Shakespeare." It is a reprint of the first quarto and put out by the same printer and publisher. In 1608 appeared a third quarto, reprinted from the second, but including this time the deposition scene of Act IV, scene 1, lines 154-318. Some of the copies of this quarto bear the following title-page: "*The Tragedie of King Richard the Second:* With new additions of the Parliament Sceane, and the deposing of King Richard, As it hath been lately acted by the Kinges Majesties seruantes, at the Globe. By William Shakespeare. At London, Printed by W. W. for Mathew Law, and are to be sold at his shop in Paules Church-yard, at the signe of the Foxe. 1608." (Except for the publisher and date some copies of this quarto have the same title page as the second quarto.) The fourth quarto of 1615 is a reprint of the third. The version printed in the First Folio of 1623 seems to have been taken from the last-named quarto with certain corrections. The Folio's title for the play is "The life and death of King Richard the Second." A fifth quarto appeared in 1634, based upon the First Folio text.

The terminal date for the play is supplied by the year of its publication, 1597. Certain parallels have been pointed out between Daniel's *Civil Wars,* which was entered in the Stationers' Register for October 1594, and Shakespeare's *Richard II*. Four books from Daniel's work came out in 1595, and there are a number of instances in which Shakespeare, though making no use of Daniel's language, follows him in details of the story. It would seem therefore as if *Richard II* could not have been written before 1595.

In Shakespeare's earliest work there is an abundance of rhyme, conceits, puns, and quibbles; there are generally less and less of these as his career proceeded. Because of the large proportion of them in *Richard II*, it was once thought that this play must have been written several years before 1595. But those elements in the drama in this case seem particularly allied to the tone of the work and the persons who give utterance to them. The artifice with which Richard speaks seems part of the author's depiction of his character.

The chief source for this history play was Raphael Holinshed's *Chronicles of England, Scotland, and Ireland,* as published in its second edition (1587). Shakespeare went to this work also for the materials in the *Henry IV* plays, but in *Richard II* he adheres much more to his source than in the later histories; in our play he is often very close to Holinshed. The changes he makes have principally to do with locale and time—for example he compresses three several meetings of Parliament into one. The characterization of Richard is, of course, Shakespeare's own; he alters John of Gaunt from a violent egotist into a splendid example of patriotism at its best; Holinshed's York is colorless; Shakespeare has made him a man of dimension; Bolingbroke has been painted in colors less alienating than he has in the *Chronicle,* and his conduct toward Richard and his enemies has been made less ruthless; In *Richard II* Mowbray figures more sympathetically, and Aumerle is seen among Richard's partisans.

From Daniel, Shakespeare seems to have adopted the following alterations of historical fact: the queen, who was actually a child of eleven, is transformed into an adult; Bolingbroke is made to woo the populace; Richard and Bolingbroke enter London side by side; Exton takes up Bolingbroke's desire to be rid of Richard.

A few minor details may have been inspired by Hall's *Chronicle* and one by Stow's *Annals*. Of Shakespeare's own invention are the other women; Act II, scene 1, lines 1-146; Act III, scene 4 (a wonderful inspiration); and the presence of the Groom in Act V, scene 5.

Richard II
in Queen Elizabeth's Time

There had been at least two plays on Richard during Elizabeth's reign: *A Tragedy of King Richard II* (1591), which opens with the king's marriage and ends with the murder of Gloucester, and *The Life and Death of Jack Straw* (1593), which concentrates on the peasant rebellion of 1381—both plays being still extant. In addition, Henslowe's *Diary* mentions a play by Wilson, Dekker, Drayton, and Chettle, named "Perce of Extone"; and there is a record of a lost play apparently on Richard's reign, which was performed April 30, 1611 at the Globe, and which may or may not have been by that time an old play.

Shakespeare's play is thought to have suddenly figured in the trial of Essex for treason early in 1600. Some follower of Essex had hired the Lord Chamberlain's Company to present the drama dealing with "the deposyng and kyllyng of Kyng Richard the second."—the intention being, so the charge ran, to stir the people to revolt against Elizabeth; the actors had protested, when approached, that the play was "so old & so long out of vse" that it would draw only a small audience; a fee of 40 shilling "more then their ordynary for yt," however, had silenced the objections, and the play had been given at the Globe on the very eve of Essex's rebellion. That it was generally understood that there was an analogy between Richard's situation and the threat to Elizabeth is evidenced by the fact that the abdication scene (Act IV) was omitted, as already stated, from the first two quartos; not until after the Queen had died did it appear at last in the third quarto (1608).

Elizabeth herself was well aware of the analogy, as is reported in a conversation she had with William Lambard during her last year of life. She said to him: "I am Richard II, know ye not that?" Referring to Essex, he replied: "Such a wicked imagination was

3

determined and attempted by a most unkind Gent., the most adorned creature that ever your Majestie made." She added: "He that will forget God, will also forget his benefactors; this tragedy was played 40 times in the open streets and houses."

The Historical Background
of the Play

Richard II (1367-1400), born at Bordeaux, was the son of Edward III's eldest son, the famous Black Prince. After the death of his father, Richard was created Prince of Wales (November, 1376). Edward III died in 1377, and Richard was crowned as his successor. Since he was so young there developed a rivalry among his uncles; these years were further aggravated by the wars and the Black Death. An uprising of the peasants (1381) under Wat Tyler threatened the establishment, when the rebels seized London. In this crisis Richard proved himself extraordinarily capable for a boy in his dealings with them, and when Wat Tyler was killed he managed to disperse the peasants.

The King now took part actively in the nation's affairs. Parliament had appointed as his leading ministers the Earl of Arundel and Michael de la Pole (1382). Richard could not bear Arundel and dismissed him (1383). He retained Pole as chancellor and created him Earl of Suffolk; Pole was a man of great ability. Unhappily, the King also distributed honors among others who did not deserve them; nothing caused more resentment than his elevation of his favorite, young Robert de Vere, to Marquess of Dublin and Duke of Ireland.

In 1383 Richard married the daughter of Emperor Charles IV, Anne of Bohemia (1366-1394); he was sixteen and she a year older. During their nine years together they were apparently very happy.

In the meantime his developing taste for excessive luxury and his self-indulgent fits of anger began to alienate many who had liked him. Gloucester, with Arundel's support, attacked Richard's advisers in Parliament (1386) and more than hinted that a deposing of the King was in the offing. Through Gloucester's influence Richard's closest friends were either executed or exiled, and for a

5

while it appeared that the King had accepted the loss of all real authority (1388). But he now countered by dismissing Gloucester's supporters from the offices they held and by 1390 had restored his own popularity. The return of his uncle, John of Gaunt, from Spain acted effectively as a deterrent upon Gloucester's ambition.

The death of his queen (1394) was a great sorrow to Richard, and he sought relief by heading an expedition to Ireland, where no English monarch had been for some two hundred years. He also entered into negotiations with France with the object of achieving peace with that country; the agreement included his marriage to Charles VI's daughter, Isabella, a child of seven. Gloucester was busy fomenting difficulties again by opposing the peace (1397). Later that year Richard suddenly ordered the arrest of Gloucester, Arundel, and Warwick. At this juncture the King was supported by Bolingbroke and Nottingham. At Calais by Richard's command Gloucester was put to death in prison by smothering. Arundel was condemned in Parliament and sent to his execution, and his brother, the Archbishop of Canterbury, was exiled. Richard elevated Bolingbroke to Duke of Hereford, and Nottingham to Duke of Norfolk, with the bestowal of estates upon them.

Now absolute monarch, Richard had free rein for his extravagance, which necessitated new and newer taxes. In vengeance against those who had killed his good friends, he persuaded Bolingbroke to accuse Norfolk of treasonable language (1398). Norfolk denied the allegation, and challenged his accuser to a judicial duel. At the last minute Richard forbade them to fight and banished both of them. The next year the King sailed again to Ireland to put down a new revolt there (1399). He left England in the conviction that he had rid himself of everyone he needed fear.

During his absence, the exiled Bolingbroke landed at Ranvenspur with a small army of exiles and mercenaries, with the pretense that he had come to claim the title and the estates of his deceased father, John of Gaunt. Dissatisfied with the wilfulness of Richard's rule, the Earl of Northumberland and the other noblemen of the North at once joined Bolingbroke, and in a matter of a few days he was master of England (July 1399).

Quickly returning, Richard landed at Milford Haven—to learn that his men had deserted him on all sides. He had a large enough force to contest the usurpation of the crown, or he could have sought asylum with his father-in-law in France. Instead, he fled from his army during the night into the mountains of Wales. If it was his hope to find fresh support, he was doomed to disappointment. Henry Bolingbroke had seized Chester and was advancing against Richard with a great army, whose presence paralyzed the support of Richard's well-wishers.

On August 19, 1399 Richard surrendered to Bolingbroke, his cousin, on the stipulation that if he should agree to abdicate the throne, his life would be spared. Treated with indignity, he was forced to ride behind the victor into London. Foolishly, Richard signed a deed of abdication in the Tower on September 30, admitting himself to be "useless." The document was read to Parliament and the throne declared vacant.

Though his claim to the crown was none of the best, Bolingbroke had all the power of the military behind him. He was, indeed, the eldest in line of descent *after* Richard, yet there were those with stronger legal rights. Edward III's second son was Lionel of Clarence, and from him was descended the six-year-old Edmund, Earl of March, whom the late King had declared his heir if he should die childless. (Bolingbroke's father, John of Gaunt, was the *third* son of Edward III.) When Bolingbroke claimed the throne, however, not a voice was heard in opposition. The Lords and Commons voted him King, and he was crowned on October 13, 1399. Faithless to his oath, he had Richard placed in solitary confinement under the most wretched of conditions, and impeached Richard's followers of treason. It is said that it was by his command that Richard died in his cell at Pontefract Castle on February 7, 1400—a victim of murder. But it has also been said that he probably died from the rigors of his imprisonment during the terrible winter. Rumor was rife that he had escaped from the Castle. Many years after Richard's death an impostor was still being sheltered by the government in Scotland. There is no doubt that it was Richard himself who was buried without ceremony at King's Langley. Henry V had the body transferred with honor to Westminster in 1413.

C. L. Kingsford has said of the historic Richard: He "is a character of strange contradictions. It is difficult to reconcile the precocious boy of 1381 with the wayward and passionate youth of the next few years . . . It is impossible to believe that the apparent indifference which he showed in his fall was the mere acting of a part. His violent outbursts of passion perhaps give the best clue to a mercurial and impulsive nature, easily elated and depressed. He had real ability, and in his Irish policy, and in the preference which he gave to it over continental adventure, showed a statemanship in advance of his time. But this, in spite of his lofty theory of kingship, makes it all the more difficult to explain his extravagant bearing in his prosperity. His fall was due to the triumph of national right over absolute government, but it was his personal conduct which made it inevitable. In appearance Richard was tall and handsome, if effeminate. He had some literary tastes, which were shown in fitful patronage of Chaucer, Gower and Froissart. His fancy for splendid dress may have been due to an artistic sense, which found better expression in his great buildings of Westminster Hall and Abbey."

The English "History" Play

The history, or, as it is sometimes called, the chronicle play, is a type of drama almost exclusively English and was in great vogue among Elizabethan audiences.

With the accession of the first Tudor king, Henry VII, the Renaissance by degrees made itself felt in England. One of its by products was an intensification of the sense of nationalism, and one of the by products of English nationalism was a new fascination with English history. There was on hand a steady supply of conscientious chroniclers, very often the authors of voluminous works, to satisfy this interest—among others, William Caxton, Edward Hall, John Foxe, Richard Grafton, John Stow, William Camden, the authors of *The Mirror for Magistrates,* and Raphael Holinshed, to list only a few.

With the victory over the Spanish Armada (1588), English patriotism soared to new heights, and there was a large public eager to read newer accounts of the country's history and tributes to the land, its monarchs, and its heroes. Worthy of mention is William Warner's *Albion's England,* expanded over the years to sixteen books; Samuel Daniel's *The Civil Wars between the Two Houses of Lancaster and York;* Michael Drayton's *Barons' Wars in the Reign of Edward the Second, England's Heroical Epistles, Polyolbion,* and *The Ballad of Agincourt.*

But the theatre, at least in London, was the most popular of all forms of literary entertainment, and here English patriotism expressed itself chiefly in the enormous popularity of the "history" play. Fifteen years elapsed between the victory over the Armada and the death of Queen Elizabeth; in that period about two hundred history plays were written and produced in London. What this species of drama meant to audiences can be glimpsed from Thomas Nashe's tribute to it in his *Pierce Penniless His Supplication to the Devil* (1592). "How would it have joyed brave Talbot (the terror of the French) to think that after he had lain two

9

hundred years in his tomb, he should triumph again on the stage and have his bones new embalmed with the tears of ten thousand spectators at least (at several times), who in the tragedian that represents his person imagine they behold him fresh bleeding."

The history play represented on the boards some era of British history, and pleased the audiences best when there were plenty of battle scenes, plenty of bloodshed, exchanges of insults and defiances between leaders of opposing sides, and a display of armies marching on and off the stage, together with enough swordplay, falling of the wounded, etc. It was by rule a loose compound of elements proper both to tragedy and comedy, held together by the march of historical events.

Aside from their patriotic fervor, the Elizabethan audiences had another important reason for their interest in their history plays. The harrowing memory of thirty terrible years of civil war of the century before was still fresh enough for Englishmen to shudder at the possibility of another. Henry VII, the first Tudor, had come to the throne on claims that were fairly shaky; a century had established the Tudor title—though the period of Mary Tudor had raised a new menace of civil turmoil out of that queen's attempts to bring the country back to Catholicism; but Queen Elizabeth had never married, and as her increasing age placed her having a direct heir beyond the resources of nature, the question of what might follow upon her death became increasingly a pressing one. As early as 1562 the first English tragedy, *Gorboduc,* told a story from Holinshed which was an admonition on the troubles bound to ensue when the regal succession is left in doubt. Edward Hall's history, too, opens with a solemn warning: "What mischief hath insurged in realms by intestine division, what depopulation hath ensued in countries by civil dissension, what detestable murder hath been committed in cities by separate factions, and what calamity hath ensued in famous regions by domestic discord and unnatural controversy, Rome hath felt, Italy can testify, France can bear witness, Beaume [Bohemia] can tell, Scotland may write, Denmark can show, and especially this noble realm of England can apparently declare and make demonstration."

The stability which most Britishers sought depended chiefly upon the monarch, as they understood the problem. If the monarch was wise, good, and strong, peace and prosperity were assured; if he was foolish, wicked, and weak, everything went to ruin. Calvinists and Roman Catholics, it is true, though bitterly opposed to each other, had one belief in common: they were no friends to their monarch's absolutism; but Calvinists and Catholics were in a small minority in Elizabethan England. Queen Elizabeth administered her country with a tolerance and perspective far in advance of what was usual in most countries in Europe, and it is not surprising therefore that the majority willingly submitted to an absolutism that ensured social tranquility and did comparatively little to tyrannize over their private lives.

Shakespeare's History Plays

Shakespeare's history plays, with the exception of *King John*, form something of a complete cycle of English history: *Richard II —1 Henry IV—2 Henry IV—Henry V—1 Henry VI—2 Henry VI— 3 Henry VI—Richard III*. He began this cycle in the middle (the three *Henry VI* plays and *Richard III* in that order) and later started upon the first half with *Richard II*.

There is something to be remarked about all these monarchs, with the notable exception of Henry V. They are all unsuccessful as kings, and their failure demonstrates the unhappiness visited upon the kingdom when the ruler is weak or evil. Henry VI, a saintly man, completely lacks the force of character to deal with the crises arising in his time; Richard III is an unmitigated villain, one of the most unprincipled Shakespeare ever drew; John is also a wicked man, and a coward to boot; Richard II is an over-imaginative, wilful, petulant, and self-dramatizing poet totally unsuited to his place; and Henry IV is a strong man, but suspicious and ungrateful towards those who have helped him most. It is only Henry V, whom we meet as Hal in *Henry IV,* who is depicted, as Holinshed too described him, as a prince of "virtues notable" and "qualities most praiseworthy," the very "pattern in princehood," though it would seem that Shakespeare was most impressed with Holinshed's designation of him as "a prince whom all men loved." In the reigns of the other monarchs Shakespeare shows only public dissatisfaction, civil contention, and anarchic discontents.

The two *Henry IV* plays are remarkable, as distinguished from Shakespeare's predecessors' and his own history plays, by the large amount of non-historical material, in the comic scenes in which Falstaff and his fellow-rogues figure. The result in these two plays is a feeling of variety unmatched in the other history plays, as well as a gratifying mixture of the serious and the droll. In *Richard II* there is hardly anything comic at all.

12

Richard II and
Marlowe's *Edward II*

The finest history play written by any of Shakespeare's predecessors for the London stage was Marlowe's *Edward II*. That Shakespeare was influenced in a general way by that play when he was writing *Richard II* will be obvious to the reader of both. Both plays center almost entirely around the king of the title; both kings almost wilfully throw away their rule by some species of personal intemperance. But the analogy almost ends there. Edward is the portrait of a homosexual who neglects his wife and alienates his noblemen by doting on his favorites and elevating them to high posts in the realm despite their humble origins. Richard, despite the attempts of some critics to make him out a homosexual, is not one; he never deserts his wife, and his favorites seem merely to be men who encourage him in the pleasures and luxuries he enjoys. The struggle in *Edward II* is between the King and his nobles; in *Richard II* it is between the king and the ambitious Bolingbroke.

Not that *Richard II* is in every way superior to *Edward II* as a play. Both dramas have their weaknesses, but it must be conceded that Marlowe has evoked more compassion for the end of his Edward than Shakespeare has for his Richard. However, though both dramatists were born in the same year, Marlowe began much earlier than Shakespeare. *Edward II* is probably the best play Marlowe wrote for the theatre—it is his last. *Richard II,* on the other hand, cannot be accounted as one of Shakespeare's masterpieces, for all its merits. He was still learning his craft while he wrote it, and his art was slowly maturing. Certainly, even if Marlowe had not been cut off at the height of his powers, there is not a shred of evidence to make us believe that his talent, great as it was, was capable of the vast and profoundly human achievement of Shakespeare at his greatest.

13

The Persons of the Play

KING RICHARD II, as seen at the beginning and later on in the play, is not quite a consistent figure. In the very first scene we are made to feel that he has not the force of personality to procure obedience to his wishes from his noblemen. He orders Bolingbroke and Mowbray to make up their differences and become friends, but he is able to make neither comply. Unable to pacify either, he goes to the opposite extreme and commands them to fight each other at Coventry. Then, at Coventry, when both are ready at the lists and anxious to begin, and Richard seems prepared to wait for the outcome of the tourney, he suddenly causes all hostilities to stop, and exiles both men. Oddly enough, he pronounces a much lighter sentence upon Bolingbroke, whom he plainly does not like, and a heavy one (life banishment) upon Mowbray, whom he has seemed to prefer. However wise these banishments may be from the standpoint of political security, the way in which Richard manages them undeniably gives the effect of capriciousness. Moreover, having been so severe with Mowbray, he again unexpectedly lessens Bolingbroke's term of exile by four years. Presently (Scene 4) he makes it clear that he does not intend forgiving Bolingbroke when the latter's term of exile is over.

Now Richard appears unattractive indeed when, hearing of the mortal illness of his uncle, John of Gaunt, he sneeringly wishes the old man a speedy demise so that he can seize upon his money. At the bedside of the dying man, Richard is shockingly callous; when Gaunt lectures him in the hope of getting him to reform his extravagant ways which are ruining the country, his nephew calls him a lunatic. When Gaunt dies Richard does not even pretend to grieve for him, but wastes no time seizing upon his uncle's possessions.

Next, the contradictions in Richard's make-up are again in evidence. Although his uncle York at last speaks out against

14

Richard's injustices, the King appoints him as his substitute during his own absence at the Irish wars, for which he sets out at once. His appointment of York would seem to bespeak Richard's ability to be fair; on the other hand, having totally brushed aside York's warning, he shows a total want of judgment in handing over the kingdom in his absence to a man who thoroughly disapproves of his conduct and from whom he has no reason to expect complete loyalty.

It is not until Richard returns from the Irish Wars (Act III, Scene 2) that he begins to win our sympathy. That is, first of all, because Bolingbroke has begun to show his true colors and is in the ascendant. And it is here that Richard starts to see himself as God's anointed whom the angels are bound to protect. Yet even now his egocentricity shocks us: misunderstanding news about his old favorites to mean that they have deserted him, whereas in fact they have paid the penalty of death for supporting him, he is quick to insult them. This is the beginning of the end for Richard; piece by piece he will lose all he has, and he is only too ready to accept defeat at once. And as he begins to fall, he begins also to unfold before us the resources of an exquisite poet. With each new mishap he half stands aside from his miseries as though he were witnessing a play in which himself is the central tragic figure. The energy he ought to use in opposing his enemies he consumes in weaving exquisite images to describe his state. Yet he has not a word of pity for those who have met their death through loyalty to him.

When Richard encounters Bolingbroke again he at once, as though he were enjoying the irony, speaks as though their roles were reversed and Bolingbroke, who has made no such effort yet, had already seized the crown. Then, when Bolingbroke is clearly in the position to deal harshly with him, Richard does not attempt either to conciliate him or say the things which would assure himself an easier future; instead, he indulges himself in the satisfaction of declaring his loathing for his triumphing enemy. Richard always can be counted upon to do what is most disadvantageous to his own welfare.

This is the kind of courage which he does possess, and we begin to pity him in earnest. He is seen at his most admirable in his brief passage with his wife (Act V, Scene 1); for her sake he tries to sound resigned, and he is concerned for her safety.

At the very end Richard shows unexpected bravery in fighting with the armed men who come to murder him, unarmed as he is, and succeeds in killing two of them. (His own death is so briefly dealt with by Shakespeare that it makes an insufficient impression on the stage.)

Shakespeare has managed to make us aware throughout of Richard's personal beauty, and, despite his egotism and early callousness, his charm and elegance. It is difficult, as we have said, to make an entity of the various facets of his character as Shakespeare has shown them. On the whole, particularly after his return from Ireland, Richard is much more like the popular misconception of Hamlet than Hamlet actually is: a prince who is more able at dramatizing his situation than encountering it in the realm of action.

HENRY BOLINGBROKE, DUKE OF HEREFORD, and later KING HENRY IV, presents a highly consistent picture of the politician who, perfect master over himself, can play whatever part circumstances call for without revealing to the world his ultimate objective. In the first act he feigns, as Richard is not able to do toward him, real affection for the latter (Scene 3). Nevertheless, on going into exile, he remembers to ingratiate himself with the common people (Scene 4), thus indicating that his thoughts are already on the crown.

Unlike Richard, whose moods are forever overflowing into words, Bolingbroke knows how to hold his tongue. When he speaks it is almost always with his objective in view. For the most part he keeps his own counsel and says comparatively little; he leaves self-revelation to Richard. He knows how to flatter without doing so grossly, as with Northumberland (Act II, Scene 3), and young Percy (same scene). He can play the hypocrite when that is useful to him, as when he kneels to his uncle York (same scene). Once he is in a position of any power, he acts swiftly and ruthlessly with those who might stand in his way, as he does, when barely returned to England, with Bushy and Green (Act III, Scene 1), not hesitating to use trumped-up charges to further his own ends. We see him once more playing the hypocrite when he upbraids Northumberland for not speaking respectfully of King Richard (Act III, Scene 3) ; yet a few minutes later he himself is threatening Richard. By the strength of his will he is able to force the King to appear before him (same scene), and then goes through the form of kneeling in feigned humility before Richard. When Richard confronts him with the truth, that he has illegally returned to England to wrest the crown from him, Bolingbroke keeps up the pretense by denying this—though not in so many words: "I come but for my own." Nevertheless, observing the weakness of his adversary, Bolingbroke is able to require the King's moving on to London.

Sparing Richard nothing, he forces him to surrender his crown publicly (Act IV). Like all cold politicians, Bolingbroke does not hesitate to use Exton to murder Richard and then, characteristically, discards him once the deed is done. Bolingbroke, in short, is in every detail the exact opposite to Richard —the sort of man cut out for success in the world of politics, who is never deterred by considerations of ethics, truth, or loyalty.

EDMUND OF LANGLEY, DUKE OF YORK, can be thought of only as a weak, blundering old man. His behavior is full of contradictions. He at first, having been given the grave responsibility of acting as Richard's substitute during the King's absence in Ireland, makes some attempt to remain faithful to his trust and loyal to the King, his nephew. But before the cold, quiet energy of Bolingbroke's resolve, his good intentions shrivel. Feeling impotent to oppose this nephew, he switches sides and loyalties to Bolingbroke. Indeed, this new allegiance suddenly becomes a religion with him, and we find it hard to accept that any man, especially considering his recent past, would go so far as to beg Bolingbroke to sentence York's own son, Aumerle, to death as a conspirator against the usurper. The suspicion is almost raised that he too is an opportunist who would sacrifice his own flesh and blood to ingratiate himself with King Henry, except that his advanced years rather suggest encroaching senility.

DUKE OF AUMERLE, York's son, remains loyal to his cousin Richard almost up to the end. It is only when his father, York, has discovered the plot against Henry and is determined to expose Aumerle as a traitor that Aumerle gives up his support of Richard—and then it is a question of submitting to the new monarch or being executed as a conspirator. He has never liked Bolingbroke (Act I, Scene 4 and Act IV).

REMAINING CHARACTERS. The other characters in the play have been rather sketchily drawn. There is some justice in Swinburne's observation that Shakespeare did not seem here "to feel for each of his characters an equal or proportionate regard; to divide and disperse his interest among the various crowd of figures which claim each its place. . . . His present interest was wholly concentrated on the single figure of Richard."

A Summary of the Action
(with a commentary upon it)

Act I

SCENE 1. King Richard's palace at Windsor: King Richard, John of Gaunt, Nobles and Attendents. Richard asks his uncle, old John of Gaunt, whether, as promised, he has brought his son Henry Bolingbroke (Duke of Hereford) to answer the accusations of Thomas Mowbray (Duke of Norfolk) and whether Bolingbroke has made his own charges against Mowbray out of malice or justifiably. Gaunt replies that his son has acted because he saw a plot intended against Richard, and that Bolingbroke is ready to appear. Richard has both contenders brought in.

They come in, both addressing the King in flattering terms. Richard asks Bolingbroke to state his case. Vowing to make good his accusation, Bolingbroke charges Mowbray with being a traitor to the King. Mowbray accuses Bolingbroke as doubly guilty of the same crime, and calls him a coward and villain (either of which terms is a challenge to fight). Bolingbroke throws down his gage as a pledge to meet the other in combat, and Mowbray accepts by picking the gage up. Asked to state the charge, Bolingbroke details it: Mowbray, he says, has received 8,000 nobles (a noble was a gold coin worth 6s. 8d.) intended for the King's soldiers which he maliciously kept for himself; has been involved in all the treasons which have been hatched against the crown for the last 18 years; and plotted the death of the late Duke of Gloucester (another uncle of the King's. Mowbray, before replying, beseeches the King, who is cousin to Bolingbroke, to judge impartially. Richard swears that he will do so. Mowbray's defense is that he distributed three-quarters of the money entrusted to him to the soldiers; the other quarter he kept as reimbursement for Richard's personal debt to him; as for Gloucester's death, he was guilty only of negligence

19

in the affair. One deed he admits: he did "lay an ambush" for the life of John of Gaunt, but has repented it and already asked Gaunt's forgiveness. Mowbray begs the King to allow him to prove his loyalty by appointing a day for the combat with Bolingbroke.

Richard will not hear of a fight and orders both men to make their peace, entreating the assistance of Gaunt. The old man bids his son throw down Mowbray's gage, which he had picked up, and Richard demands the like of Mowbray. Mowbray pleads with Richard for the right to defend his name against the slander which has been made thus public. The King then turns to his cousin and asks him to make the first overtures to peace, but he refuses.

Since the King cannot make them friends, he commands them to be ready to meet at Coventry on September 17 to settle the matter.

◆ *Commentary.*   Historically it was at Shrewsbury that Boling-broke accused Mowbray in January of 1398. Both men were summoned before a commission the next month, where each accused the other again. They were arrested to await the King's investigation. Some weeks later Richard came to Windsor to inquire into the charges. John of Gaunt, whose name came from the fact that he was born at Ghent, was 58 at this time.

In this scene, two things are already evident: Richard's inability to make his subjects obey him—it is he who is forced to change his mind—and John of Gaunt's loyalty to the King.

These are the passages from Holinshed's *Chronicles* which Shakespeare put to use in his first scene:

So it fell out, that in this parlement holden at Shrewsburie, Henrie duke of Hereford accused Thomas Mowbraie duke of Norfolke, of certeine words which he should utter in talke had betwixt them, as they rode togither latelie before betwixt London and Brainford, sounding highlie to the kings dishonor. And for further proofe thereof, he presented a supplication to the king, wherein he appealed the duke of Norfolke in field of battell, for a traitor, false and disloiall to the king, and enimie unto the realme. This supplication was red before both the dukes, in presence of the king: which doone, the duke of Norfolke tooke upon him to answer it, declaring that whatsoever the duke of Hereford had said against him other than well, he lied falselie like an untrue knight as he was. And when the king asked of the duke of Hereford what he said to it: he taking his hood off his head, said: My sovereigne lord, even as the supplication which I tooke you importeth, right so I saie for truth, that Thomas Mowbraie duke of Norfolke is a traitour, false and disloiall to your roiall maiestie, your crowne, and to all the states of your realme.

Then the duke of Norfolke being asked what he said to this, he answered: Right deere lord, with your favour that I make answer unto your coosine here, I saie (your reverence saved) that Henrie of Lancaster duke of Hereford, like a false and disloiall traitor as he is, dooth lie, in that he hath or shall say of me otherwise than well. No more said the king, we have heard inough: and herewith commanded the duke of Surric for that turne marshall of England, to arrest in his name the two dukes . . .

Now after the dissolving of the parlement at Shrewsburie, there was a daie appointed about six weeks after, for the king to come unto Windsor, to heare and to take order betwixt the two dukes, which had thus appealed ech other. There was a great scaffold erected within the castell of Windsor for the king to sit with the lords and prelats of his realm . . . The duke of Hereford appellant, and the duke of Norfolke defendant, were sent for to come & appeare before the king, sitting there in his seat of iustice. And then began sir John Bushie to speake for the king, who . . . would now heare what the parties could say one against an other, and withall the king commaunded the dukes of Aumarle and Surrie . . . to go unto the two dukes, . . . requiring them on his behalfe, to grow to some agreement: and for his part, he would be readie to pardon all that had beene said or doone amisse betwixt them, touching anie harme or dishonor to him or his realme: but they answered both assuredlie, that it was not possible to have anie peace or agreement made betwixt them.

When he heard what they had answered, he commanded that they should be brought foorthwith before his presence . . . When they were come before the king and lords, the king spake himselfe to them, willing them to agree, and make peace togither . . . The duke of Norfolke with due reverence hereunto answered it could not be so brought to passe, his honor saved. Then the king asked of the duke of Hereford, what it was he demanded of the duke of Norfolke, and what is the matter that ye can not make peace togither, and become friends?

Then stood foorth a knight; who asking and obteining licence to speake for the duke of Hereford, said; Right deare and sovereigne lord, . . . Henrie of Lancaster duke of Hereford . . . saith . . . that Thomas Mowbraie is a false and disloiall traitor to you and your roiall maiestie, and to your whole realme; and likewise the duke of Hereford saith . . . that Thomas Mowbraie duke of Norfolke hath received eight thousand nobles to pay the souldiers that keepe your towne of Calis, which he hath not doone as he ought: and furthermore . . . hath beene the occasion of all the treason that hath beene contrived in your realme for the space of these eighteene yeares, & by his false suggestions and malicious counsell, he hath caused to die and to be murdered your right deere uncle, the duke of Glocester, sonne to king Edward. Moreover, the duke of Hereford saith . . . that he will prove this with his bodie against the bodie of the said duke of Norfolke within lists. The king herewith waxed angrie, and asked the duke of Hereford, if these were his woords, who answered: Right deere lord, they are my woords . . .

There was a knight also that asked licence to speake for the duke of Norfolke, and obteining it, began to answer thus: Right deere sovereigne lord, . . . Thomas Mowbraie duke of Norfolke . . . saith . . . that all which Henrie of Lancaster hath said and declared (saving the reverence due to the king and his councell) is a lie; and the said Henrie of Lancaster hath falselie and wickedlie lied as a false and disloiall knight, and both hath beene, and is a traitor against you, your crowne, roiall maiestie, & realme. This will I prove and defend as becommeth a loiall knight to doo with my bodie against his . . .

The king then demanded of the duke of Norfolke, if these were his woords, and whether he had anie more to saie. The duke of Norfolke then answered for himselfe: Right deere sir, true it is, that I have received so much gold to paie your people of the towne of Calis; which I have doone, and I doo avouch that your towne of Calis is as well kept at your commandement as ever it was at anie time before . . . Right deere and my sovereigne lord, for the voiage that I made into France, about your marriage, I never received either gold or silver of you, nor yet for the voiage that the duke of Aumarle & I made into Almane, where we spent great treasure: Marie true it is, that once I laid an ambush to

have slaine the duke of Lancaster, that there sitteth: but never-
thelesse he hath pardoned me thereof, and there was good peace
made betwixt us, for the which I yeeld him hartie thankes. This
is that which I have to answer, and I am readie to defend my
selfe against mine adversarie . . .

   After this, when the king had communed with his councell
a little . . . the K. then caused them once againe to be asked, if
they would agree and make peace togither, but they both flatlie
answered that they would not: and withall the duke of Hereford
cast downe his gage, and the duke of Norfolke tooke it up. The
king . . . sware by saint John Baptist, that he would never seeke
to make peace betwixt them againe. And therfore sir John Bushie
in name of the king & his councell declared, that the king & his
councell had commanded and ordeined, that they should have a
daie of battell appointed them at Coventrie . . .

   In Edward Hall's *The Union of Two Noble Famelies of Lan-
castre and Yorke* (1548), which Shakespeare also knew, the point
of view is totally different. There it is said that Bolingbroke

   a prudent and politike persone, but not more politike then
   welbeloved, and yet not so welbeloved of all, . . . began to con-
   sider with hymself how that kyng Richarde his cosyn germaine
   was now brought to that trade of livyng that he litle or nothyng
   regarded the counsaill of his uncles, . . . but did all thyng at his
   pleasure . . . Wherefore on a daie beeyng in the companye of
   Thomas Mowbrey first duke of Norffolke . . . beganne to breake
   his mynde to hym . . . He desired the duke of Norffolke, whiche
   was one of the kynges privy counsaill and well heard with hym,
   to advise the kyng to turne the lefe and take a better lesson . . .
   The Duke of Norffolke . . . toke it not in goode parte, but rekened
   that he had gotten a praie by the whiche he should obtayne
   greater favor of the kyng than ever he had . . . And after when
   he had oportunite . . . was very glad . . . to declare to the kyng
   what he had heard, and to agravate and make the offence the
   greater . . .

      Kyng Richard . . . determined to here bothe the parties
   indifferently . . .

Shakespeare chose to accept Holinshed's version and make
Bolingbroke the first to bring charges. It will be noted, however,

that he uses neither Bushy to speak for Richard nor a knight to speak for the opponents, in the interest of more direct dramatic impact. He also shows Richard making a stronger appeal, than in his source, for peace between the two; thus Richard's failure here already indicates the weakness of his character. He has John of Gaunt side emphatically with the King, though in the source Gaunt is merely indicated as present during the proceedings.

We are made to feel that Bolingbroke's chief motive is to avenge the murder of Thomas of Woodstock, Duke of Gloucester, Richard's uncle and Gaunt's brother, who was assassinated at Calais in September 1397. The way Mowbray passes over that event seems to imply Richard's connivance in the matter, of which Holinshed explicity states the King was guilty. Mowbray was under orders to execute Gloucester secretly as soon as the King sent word; Mowbray, however, according to Holinshed,

> prolonged time for the executing of the kings commandement, though the king would have had it doone with all expedition, whereby the king conceived no small displeasure, and sware that it should cost the earle his life if he quickly obeied not his commandement.

To those in Shakespeare's audience, therefore, who knew their English history, Mowbray's apology,

> For Gloucester's death
> I slew him not: but to my own disgrace
> Neglected my sworn duty in that case,

while on the surface it seems to mean one thing, to Richard is an admission of failure to carry out his command in putting Gloucester to death at once.

SCENE 2. The palace of John of Gaunt: John of Gaunt and his sister-in-law, the Duchess of Gloucester. Gaunt protests that being Gloucester's brother ("the part I had in Woodstock's blood") is more than enough to stir him against Gloucester's murderers. But since punishment must lie in Richard's hands, he and the Duchess would do well to await Heaven's direction in the matter. The Duchess upbraids him for taking such a position, which would be better described as despair, and which only invites his own murder. In self-protection Gaunt must avenge his brother. But Gaunt states the acceptance of the divine right of kings; Richard is God's anointed, even though responsible for Gloucester's death: let Heaven exact vengeance.

Unable to alter his attitude, she prays that Bolingbroke may overcome Mowbray, that the weight of Mowbray's sin may break his horse's back and cause him to be thrown "headlong in the lists" at Coventry. Before leaving she sends her regards to his brother, York, with an invitation to visit her soon at Plashy (in Essex) — then decides that York had better not come, for nothing is left in her house but desolateness.

◆ *Commentary.* This little scene is what scholarship has called a "separation scene." Since there were no curtains on the Elizabethan stage, and almost no scenery, and since scene followed scene without interruption, it was Shakespeare's device to interpolate between two scenes which followed each other in dramatic idea (as, in this case, the first and third scenes of this act), a short scene, usually indefinite in the time it takes place, to enable the audience to feel a lapse in time and/or a change in place. As usual, however, Shakespeare puts the separation scene to good use. We are made to feel more strongly Gaunt's loyalty to the crown, despite the ties of blood. Later on we shall be made to understand that that loyalty is motivated above all by his concern for the welfare of England. It is his philosophy that only obedience to the King can keep the country from chaos.

There is, on the whole, no source for this scene. It is true that in the old play, *Woodstock,* on Gloucester, the Duchess briefly appears to urge York and Gaunt to take vengeance for the murder of her husband, but there is no resemblance in the way Gaunt behaves toward her proposal. Gaunt's reference to the King as God's deputy is the expression of what is a common idea in Elizabethan thought.

SCENE 3. The lists at Coventry: the Lord Marshal and the Duke of Aumerle. The Marshal informs Aumerle that Bolingbroke and Mowbray are both ready for the contest, and eager to begin it. The trumpets sound, and Richard enters with Gaunt, Bushy, Bagot, Green, and other nobles. When they have taken their places, Mowbray and a Herald come in. There follow the formalities usual on such an occasion. Richard asks the Marshal to inquire of Mowbray his name and a statement of his cause. The Marshal does so. Mowbray states his facts. The trumpet sounds again; Bolingbroke enters with his herald, and goes through the same ceremony.

Bolingbroke asks leave to kiss Richard's hand and to say his farewell to his friends. Richard comes down, embraces Bolingbroke, and warns him that should he lose the combat his death cannot, under the circumstances, be avenged. Bolingbroke does not wish to be mourned if he dies, and salutes ("regreet") Aumerle and Gaunt, and asks his father's prayers for his victory. Gaunt wishes him all success against his "pernicious" enemy. Mowbray, on his part, asserts the justice of his cause, and Richard declares his confidence in Mowbray's virtue and valor. Each combatant's herald states the cause of each once more, the trumpets sound, and the two are ready for the combat.

But suddenly Richard throws his truncheon ("warder") down as a signal that hostilities are to cease. He orders the pair back to their chairs while he announces his decision: in order to avoid civil strife which might attend this combat, he banishes both men —Bolingbroke for ten years and Mowbray for life. Mowbray protests that he has not merited this crippling blow at Richard's hands; it is terrible that he must go somewhere in the world where he can never use again his "native English," so dear to him. Richard bids him not pity himself ("be compassionate"), and requires of both men an oath, which they take, never to meet again in their exile and never to plot against their King or country. Bolingbroke asks Mowbray, now that they are both banished, to confess that he was a traitor; Mowbray swears that he never was—and that he is only too certain that Richard will rue Bolingbroke's treachery. With that Mowbray exits, to lose himself in exile.

Seeing that Gaunt is grieving, Richard, without being asked to do so, reduces the period of Bolingbroke's exile to six years. What power in a king's word, reflects Bolingbroke, that can sweep away four years in a breath. Gaunt thanks Richard, but is sure that he will not be alive to see his son again. Richard reminds Gaunt that he had agreed to the justice of his son's banishment, and will not alter the verdict. The King and his attendants leave.

Aumerle asks that Bolingbroke let him hear from him, and Gaunt tries to minimize the length of six years—let his son think he is traveling for pleasure, and concentrate on the joy of his homecoming—and goes off to accompany Bolingbroke on his way.

◆ *Commentary.* In this scene Shakespeare invented Richard's farewells to both the combatants as well as his reasons for presently exiling both; also invented are Gaunt's being the cause of the reduction of his son's term of exile and his parting with Bolingbroke.

The audience was asked to imagine that the stage represented the lists. It is to be noted that the dramatist has deliberately emphasized the conventions of such a combat. But in Holinshed it is Bolingbroke who, as the appellant, enters first. Richard's words to Mowbray, "Farewell, my lord," etc., show his partiality to him, just as his earlier words, to Bolingbroke, "Lament we may," etc., have a touch of the ironic. His harsher judgment on Mowbray is therefore the more astonishing.

In Holinshed we read that, having stopped the fight, Richard retired to consult with his advisors, and that it was Bushy who proclaimed their decisions. Holinshed does not account for the difference in the two sentences of exile, nor does Shakespeare. Holinshed also gives no reason for the reduction of Bolingbroke's period of banishment, while Shakespeare gives it a dramatic motive. It has been suggested that Gaunt's counsel on bearing exile with patience was inspired by a passage in Lyly's *Euphues* (1578), itself adapted from Plutarch.

Most critics have seen in Richard's stopping of the combat and exiling of the opponents a proof of the King's unpredictableness and unreliability; one scholar has gone so far as to assert that Richard had deliberately pre-arranged the whole affair to end this way, so that he might display his royal prerogatives. But it is seriously to be questioned that this is what Shakespeare intended. There seems no reason to question Richard's reasons—*i.e.*, that civil bloodshed might ensue from the death of either contestant, and that the only solution for the sake of peace is exile. Gaunt, himself, it will be remembered, has agreed to the justice of such a course. In short, we perhaps ought to see the action as demonstrating that Richard, having in the first scene attempted in vain to reconcile Mowbray and Bolingbroke, here acts with kingly wisdom in banishing both men. The difference in their sentences, however, having been unexplained by Holinshed, is left mysterious by Shakespeare.

These are the passages in Holinshed used by Shakespeare:

At the time appointed the king came to Coventrie, where the two dukes were readie, according to the order prescribed therein, comming thither in great arraie. . . . The king caused a sumptuous scaffold or theater, and roiall listes there to be erected and prepared. The sundaie before they should fight, after dinner the duke of Hereford came to the king . . . to take his leave of him. The morrow after, being the daie appointed for the combat, . . . came the duke of Norfolke to the court to take leave likewise of the king. The duke of Hereford armed him in his tent, . . . and the duke of Norfolke, in a beautiful house . . .

The duke of Aumarle that daie, being high constable of England, and the duke of Surrie marshall, placed themselves betwixt them, well armed and appointed . . . About the houre of prime came to the barriers of the listes, the duke of Hereford . . . The constable and marshall came to the barriers, demanding of him what he was, he answered; I am Henrie of Lancaster duke of Hereford, which am come hither to doo mine indevor against Thomas Mowbraie, duke of Norfolke, as a traitor untrue to God, the king, his realme, and me. Then incontinentlie he sware upon the holie evangelists, that his quarrell was true and iust, and upon that point he required to enter the lists. Then he put up his sword, . . . and putting downe his visor, made a crosse on his horsse, and set him downe in a chaire of greene velvet, at the one end of the lists, and there reposed himselfe, abiding the comming of his adversarie.

Soone after him, entred into the field with great triumph, king Richard accompanied with all the peeres of the realme. The king had there above ten thousand men in armour, least some fraie or tumult might rise amongst his nobles. . . . A king at armes made open proclamation, prohibiting all men in the name of the king . . . to enterprise or attempt to approach or touch any part of the lists . . . An other herald cried; Behold here Henrie of Lancaster duke of Hereford appellant, which is entred into the lists roiall to doo his devoir against Thomas Mowbraie, duke of Norfolke defendant, upon paine to be found false and recreant.

The duke of Norfolke hovered on horssebacke at the entrie of the lists, . . . and when he had made his oth before the constable and marshall that his quarrell was iust and true, he entred the field manfullie, saieng alowd: God aid him that hath the right, and then he departed from his horsse, & sate him downe in his chaire . . . The lord marshall . . . delivered the one speare himselfe to the duke of Hereford, and sent the other unto the duke of Norfolke by a knight. Then the herald proclamed that the traverses & chaires of the champions should be remooved, commanding them on the kings behalfe to mount on horssebacke, & addresse themselves to the battell and combat.

The duke of Hereford was quicklie horssed, and . . . the duke of Norfolke was not fullie set forward, when the king cast downe his warder, and the heralds cried, Ho, ho. Then the king caused their speares to be taken from them, and commanded them to repaire againe to their chaires, where they remained two long houres, while the king and his councell deliberatlie consulted what order was best to be had in so weightie a cause. Finallie, . . . sir John Bushie the kings secretarie read the sentence and determination of the king and his councell, . . . the effect whereof was, that Henrie duke of Hereford should within fifteene daies depart out of the realme, and not to return before the terme of ten yeares were expired, . . . and this upon paine of death; and that Thomas Mowbraie duke of Norfolke, bicause he had sowen sedition in the relme by his words, should likewise avoid the realme, and never to returne againe into England, nor approach the borders or confines thereof upon paine of death . . .

When these iudgements were once read, the king called before him both the parties, and made them to sweare that the one should never come in place where the other was, willinglie; nor keepe any companie to gither in any forren region; which oth they both received humblie, and so went their waies. The duke of Norfolke departed sorowfullie out of the relme into Almanie, and at the last came to Venice, where he for thought and melancholie deceassed: for he was in hope . . . that he should have beene borne out in the matter by the king . . . The duke of Hereford tooke his leave of the king at Eltham, who there released foure yeares of his banishment: so he tooke his iornie over into Calis, and from thence went into France, where he remained.

SCENE 4. The Court: Richard enters at one door with Bagot and Green, the Duke of Aumerle at another. Richard asks Aumerle about Bolingbroke's departure; Aumerle replies that he left the exile at the next highway, was not sorry to see him go, and would willingly add years to his banishment. Richard reminds him that Bolingbroke is cousin to both of them [Quarto reading: "He is our cousin's cousin"—i.e., *your* cousin too; Folio reading: "He is our Cosin (Cosin) ." The meaning is about the same.], but adds that it is doubtful that when he returns from exile he will be allowed to see his kinsmen. Richard then remarks on how, upon departing, Bolingbroke courted the favor of the common people, as though he were trying to win them away from their king.

Green changes the conversation to the rebellion in Ireland, which calls for immediate measures. Richard announces that he will go there in person; the royal coffers being empty, he is forced to sell to the highest bidder the income from taxes ("to farm our royal realm") , and to levy special sums among the wealthy.

Bushy comes in to say that John of Gaunt is very ill and asks for the King's immediate visit. Richard hopes that Gaunt will die soon; his money will come in handy to help finance the Irish campaign. Richard's friends cry, "Amen."

◆ *Commentary.* Aumerle's hostility toward Bolingbroke is Shakespeare's invention.

This is the first occasion that Richard has become aware of Bolingbroke's wooing of the populace, and we understand why he suggests that he may never allow his cousin's return.

It will be noted that in this scene, where Richard is not being heard by his court or an audience, he speaks without flourish or embellishment, and indeed seems rather to assume a sneering tone. He is certainly seen here at his least attractive, and his callousness at his uncle's impending death is shocking.

The Irish campaign, which will figure so fatefully in Richard's future, is now mentioned for the first time.

These are the passages in Holinshed relevant to our scene:

A woonder it was to see what number of people ran after him [Bolingbroke] in everie towne and street where he came, before he tooke the sea, lamenting and bewailing his departure, as who would saie, that when he departed, the onelie shield, defense, and comfort of the commonwealth was vaded and gone.* . . .

Many blanke charters were devised, and brought into the citie [London], which manie of the substantiall and wealthie citizens were faine to seale, to their great charge. And the like charters were sent abroad into all shires within the realme, whereby great grudge and murmuring arose among the people.** . . .

The common brute [rumor] ran, that the king had set to farme the realme of England, unto sir William Scroope earle of Wiltshire, and then treasuror of England, to sir John Bushie, sir John Bagot, and sir Henry Greene . . . King Richard being destitute of treasure to furnish such a princelie port as he mainteined, borrowed great summes of monie of manie of the great lords and peeres of his realme, . . . promising them in good earnest . . . that he would repaie the monie so borrowed at a daie appointed: which notwithstanding he never paid.

Act II

SCENE 1. Ely House: John of Gaunt, the Duke of York, who is sick, and attendants. This scene presents a problem not infrequent in Shakespeare, that of "double time." At the conclusion of the first act we have read that John of Gaunt is dying and wishes to see Richard at once, and it is therefore natural to assume that this scene must occur on the same day. Yet we are informed in this scene that Bolingbroke, who went into exile earlier that day, is on his way back from France; also that Richard has prevented his marrying in that country. Bolingbroke is therefore made to begin his return to England before his lands have been confiscated. Moreover, Gaunt has been allowed no time in which to become mortally ill. These difficulties, however, are such as would not occur to one during the performance of the play, and Shakespeare's

---

*Note that here it is the people who woo Bolingbroke. Shakespeare has him woe them.

**Shakespeare makes this collecting of monies a means of financing the Irish war.

first concern was dramatic effectiveness, which was achieved by compressing time when it so suited him.

Gaunt asks whether Richard will heed his summons: he wishes to advise him on his thoughtless conduct. York doubts that the King can be taught good counsel. Perhaps, Gaunt suggests, Richard might weigh the words of a dying man; York insists that the King is too much engulfed in flattery and the pursuit of novelty to hear what Gaunt might say. Inspired like a prophet, Gaunt, after a magnificent patriotic outburst (in lines that have become celebrated, beginning: "This royal throne of kings"), denounces the present state of corruption in England, the product of Richard's luxurious and wanton living.

Richard, the Queen, Aumerle, Bushy, Green, Bagot, Ross, and Willoughby come in, and as they enter York counsels his brother Gaunt to speak mildly to the King, for young men are likely to become even more hot-headed when rebuked. Gaunt talks bitterly of the cause of his illness, his son's exile, but warns Richard that he is dying too, his deathbed being England, where the King lies sick in reputation, and has as his physicians those who first made him ill: his thousand flatterers. If Edward III had foreseen how his grandson was going to lay waste the family, he would have made sure that Richard would never have inherited the crown.

As Gaunt's severity mounts, Richard interrupts him to call him a lunatic who dares presume upon his illness to speak words that would otherwise cost him his life. Gaunt proudly asks not to be spared, since Richard has already made merry over the blood of one uncle (Gloucester). His parting words are a curse upon Richard: "Live in thy shame, but die not shame with thee!" As for himself, he asks to be taken to his bed: he has nothing left to live for. As he is carried out, Richard wishes him a speedy death.

York tries to mollify the King by pleading Gaunt's illness and age; he is sure that Gaunt loves Richard as much as he does his own banished son. Pretending to misunderstand, Richard agrees that Gaunt loves him as much as Bolingbroke does, and he himself loves them as little.

Northumberland enters to announce Gaunt's death. Richard has not a word of regret or sorrow, and begins to speak of the Irish wars. To help finance them he declares that he will seize all of Gaunt's property. York, who has been tactful toward his nephew, can no longer hold his tongue, though he has said nothing about Gloucester's death or Bolingbroke's banishment or Richard's interference in the latter's marriage. York is the last of Edward III's sons. He pays tribute to Richard's father, the late Prince of Wales, as a truly princely man; though Richard looks like him, the Prince of Wales was not an enemy to friends, was guiltless of his kindred's blood, and fierce only with their enemies. Why should the King now wish to seize what belongs to banished Bolingbroke? Does not Bolingbroke deserve to inherit his father's property? If Richard commit such an injustice, he will only invite a thousand dangers on his own head and lose countless friends. [To "sue his livery" refers to the fact that Gaunt's lands would revert to the king's hands, under the law, until Bolingbroke would prove that he was of age to inherit them; having recovered his inheritance, the heir would then do homage to his sovereign.] Richard remains ruthless, however, despite the warning. York leaves, unwilling to be a witness to such wickedness.

Richard sends Bushy to Scrope, Lord Treasurer of England, to come to Ely House at once to seize upon Gaunt's effects. Tomorrow the King leaves for Ireland; in his absence he appoints York lord governor of England because he is a just man. The court goes out. Ross indicates his grief over Bolingbroke's losses; Northampton and Willoughby encourage him to speak out to them. Northampton thinks Richard the victim of evil flattering friends; Ross observes that the King has lost the support of the commons and nobility by his levying of taxes and his fines; Northampton adds that he cannot pretend it has been because of wars, for Richard has fought none—he has spent more in peace than his forebears did on wars, and is surrounded by dissoluteness. Richard is degenerate, he continues, but there is hope in the news that Bolingbroke and some supporters have been outfitted by the Duke of Bretagne with ships and men, and are headed for England, waiting only for Richard's departure for Ireland. If the others will redeem the country from the decay into which it has fallen, let them quickly go with Northampton to meet Bolingbroke at Ravenspurgh. They at once agree to do so.

◆ *Commentary.* Gaunt having been shown as loyal to the crown even against the dictates of natural affection, his denunciation of Richard's reign strikes the audience with the ring of solemn truth. The King's own callousness to his uncle's death and his cheap cynicism and mockery of the dying man's warning bring our opinion of him to its lowest ebb. His failure to heed the logic of the moderate York sounds an overtone of the sad end he is preparing for himself. On the other hand, his appointment of that same York as his substitute while he is away in Ireland, while it might indicate fair-mindedness, shows, under the circumstances, a total want of judgment. What loyalty can he hope from York after he has ignored his wise predictions?

The nobility of Gaunt's tribute to England has justly made it a famous passage, much remembered by Englishmen in times of national stress. But Gaunt's other lines (e.g., his "O, how that name" speech) are often marred by the plays upon words and the sort of dramatically inept verbal cleverness characteristic of Shakespeare's earliest manner.

These are the passages in Holinshed which Shakespeare used:

At his [Bolingbroke's] comming into France, king Charles hearing the cause of his banishment . . . received him gentlie, and him honorablie intertéined, in so much that he had by favour obtained in mariage the onelie daughter of the duke of Berrie, uncle to the French king, if king Richard had not beene a let in that matter, who being thereof certified, sent the earle of Salisburie with all speed into France, both to surmize by untrue suggestion, heinous offenses against him, and also to require the French king that in no wise he would suffer his cousine to be matched in mariage with him that was so manifest an offendor....

1399 . . . In this meane time, the duke of Lancaster departed out of this life at the bishop of Elies place in Holborne. . . . The death of this duke gave occasion of increasing more hatred in the people of this realme toward the king, for he seized into his hands all the goods that belonged to him, and also received all the rents and revenues of his lands, which ought to have descended unto the duke of Hereford by lawfull inheritance, in revoking his letters patents, which he had granted to him before, by vertue whereof he might make his attornies generall to sue liverie for him, of any maner of inheritances or possessions that might from thenceforth fall unto him, and that his homage might be respited, with making reasonable fine: whereby it was evident, that the king meant his utter undooing . . .

The duke of Yorke was therewith sore mooved, who before this time, had borne things with so patient a mind as he could, though the same touched him verie neere, as the death of his brother the duke of Glocester, the banishment of his nephue the said duke of Hereford, and other mo iniuries in great number, which for the slipperie youth of the king, he passed over for the time, and did forget aswell as he might. But now perceiving that neither law, iustice nor equitie could take place, where the kings wilfull will was bent upon any wrongfull purpose, he considered that the glorie of the publike wealth of his countrie must needs decaie, by reason of the king his lacke of wit, and want of such as would (without flatterie) admonish him of his dutie: and therefore he thought it the part of a wise man to get him in time to a resting place, and to leave the following of such an anadvised capteine, as with a leden sword would cut his owne throat . . .

The king departed toward Bristow, from thence to passe into Ireland, leaving . . . for his lieutenant generall in his absence his uncle the Duke of Yorke . . .

Now whilest he was thus occupied [in Ireland] in devising how to reduce them into subiection, . . . diverse of the nobilitie, as well prelates as other and like wise manie of the magistrates and rulers of the cities, townes and communaltie, here in England, perceiving dailie how the realme drew to utter ruine, not like to be recovered . . . whilest king Richard lived and reigned . . . devised . . . to send and signifie by letters unto duke Henrie . . . requiring him with all convenient speed to conveie himselfe into England, promising him all their aid, power and assistance, if he expelling K. Richard, as a man not meet for the office he bare, would take upon him the scepter, rule and obedience of his native land and religion.

He therefore being thus called upon by messengers and letters from his freends, and cheeflie through the earnest persuasion of Thomas Arundell, late archbishop of Canterburie, who . . . had beene remooved from his see, and banished the realme by king Richards means, got him down to Britaine*, together with

*Brittany.

the said archbishop, where he was ioyfullie received of the duke and duchesse, and found such freendship at the dukes hands, that there were certeine ships rigged, and made readie for him, at a place in base Britaine called Le port blanc . . . He tooke the sea, togither with the said archbishop of Canturburie, and his nephue Thomas Arundell, sonne and heire to the late earle of Arundell . . . There were also with him, Reginald lord Cobham, sir Thomas Erpingham, and sir Thomas Ramston knights, John Norburie, Robert Waterton, & Frances Coint esquires: few else were there, for (as some write) he had not past fifteene lances, . . . that is to saie, men of armes, furnished and appointed as the use then was. Yet other write, that the duke of Britaine delivered unto him eight ships well furnished . . . He approching to the shore, did not streight take land, but lay hovering aloofe . . .

It will be remarked that Shakespeare invented Richard's visit to Gaunt as well as York's personal reproof.

The reader of Holinshed's account of the reign of Richard might well have been astonished at the transformation of his character in Shakespeare's hands. In the *Chronicles* Gaunt figures as a violent self-centered seeker of power, not Shakespeare's loyal patriot and seer. It has been suggested that Shakespeare took some hint for Gaunt's illness and ill-bodings for the kingdom from Berners' translation of Froissart's *Chronicles,* but the argument is not conclusive. Shakespeare's imagination was surely equal to the invention.

SCENE 2. Windsor Castle: the Queen, Bushy and Bagot. Bushy bids the Queen give up her heavy mood, as she has promised Richard to do, and be cheerful. She can account for her sadness on two grounds: Richard's absence (he has gone off to Ireland) and a foreboding of sorrow to come—it is a "nameless woe" she feels. Green comes in with the news that Bolingbroke has landed in England at Ravenspurgh. Worse yet, Northumberland and his son Harry (Percy), Ross, Beaumond, Willoughby, and many other powerful friends have hastened to join him. These men have already been publicly proclaimed traitors, with the result that the Earl of Worcester has broken his staff of office and hastened to join the rebels. The Queen understands now why she had premonitions of evil.

York enters in armor. He deplores Richard's being away and that the care of the kingdom has been left to a man as aged and weak as himself. A servant comes in with the news that York's son, the Duke of Aumerle, has gone with Richard to Ireland, and also that York's sister-in-law, the Duchess of Gloucester, is dead. At this bitter information and with the weight of responsibility for the kingdom on him, York wishes that the King had arranged his assassination as he had York's brother's, Gloucester. He is mightily disturbed over the situation in which he finds himself. Where will he find money to war against Bolingbroke? Moreover, both Richard and Bolingbroke are equally related to him; his loyalty is sworn to Richard, but how can he with conscience oppose Bolingbroke, whom Richard has wronged?

York leads the Queen out to take her to a place of safety. Bushy, Green, and Bagot know they are in some danger because of their closeness to the King. As for the commons, they will follow wherever profit comes to them; they are not likely to love Richard for emptying their purses. Green and Bushy plan to flee to Bristol Castle to join the Earl of Wiltshire; Bagot will proceed to Ireland to be with Richard, and as he says farewell to the other two, he senses that they will never meet again. They realize that York is in too hopeless a dilemma to expect that he can stand up against the King's enemies.

◆ *Commentary.* Shakespeare, like Daniel, has altered the historical Queen from a mere child to a young woman, and the scene between her and Richard's favorites is Shakespeare's invention. The Queen is touchingly pathetic. Taking bits from Holinshed here and there, Shakespeare placed the news of Bolingbroke's return, the adherence of many noblemen to his cause, and the proclaiming of Northumberland as a traitor in Green's mouth, and that of the Duchess of Gloucester's death in the Servant's. York's behavior in this scene is an elaboration of certain hints in Holinshed, but is largely Shakespeare's own portrayal of York's character as confused and weak.

Bushy's "perspectives" (l. 18) is a reference to a popular toy, the perspective picture, fashioned of paper in such a way that it gave one impression when viewed from the front ("rightly") and another when viewed from an angle (awry"). The Queen's "though on thinking on no thought I think" (l. 31) means "though I attempt to think of nothing." "Conceit" (l. 33), a word that appears frequently in Shakespeare, usually means "fancy." Ravenspurgh, on the river Humber, was once an important port. Note the many plays upon words in the earlier part of this scene (e.g., on *hope,* lines 42 seq.).

Shakespeare follows Holinshed in having Bagot go to Ireland, but by the next scene he has apparently forgotten for there (l. 164) we find him with Bushy at Bristol.

These are the relevant passages in Holinshed:

> The duke of Yorke was a man rather coveting to live in pleasure, than to deale with much businesse, and the weightie affairs of the realme . . .

> The lord treasuror, Bushie, Bagot, and Greene, perceiving that the commons would cleave unto, and take part with, the duke [Bolingbroke], slipped awaie, leaving the lord governour of the realme, and the lord chancellor to make what shift they could for themselves: Bagot got him to Chester, and so escaped to Ireland; the other fled to the castell of Bristow, in hope there to be in safetie. The duke of Lancaster, after that he had coasted alongst the shore a certeine time, & had got some intelligence how the peoples minds were affected towards him, landed about the beginning of Julie in Yorkshire, at a place called Ravenspur, betwixt Hull and Bridlington . . . : . . . he was so ioyfullie received of the lords, knights, and gentlemen of those parts, that he found means (by their helpe) forthwith to assemble a great number of people, that were willing to take his part. . . .

> At his comming unto Doncaster, the earle of Northumberland and his sonne, sir Henrie Persie, wardens of the marches against Scotland, with the earle of Westmerland, came unto him, where he sware unto those lords, that he would demand no more, but the lands that were to him descended by inheritance from his father, and in right of his wife.

SCENE 3. Gloucestershire: Bolingbroke and Northumberland (with an army). Though the way from Ravenspurgh has been long and weary, Bolingbroke, says Northumberland, has made it delectable by his sweet discourse. Henry Percy comes in and is introduced to Bolingbroke by his father, Northumberland. The young man reports that Northumberland's brother, Worcester, has resigned his office of Lord High Steward, dismissed the King's household staff, has left the court because Northumberland has been proclaimed traitor, and has gone to Ravenspurgh to join Bolingbroke. Northumberland asks his son whether he does not remember Bolingbroke; but young Percy does not remember ever having met him. "Then learn to know him now," responds his father, "this is the Duke." Percy offers his services to Bolingbroke, who vows to reward the youth for his friendship.

They are near Berkeley Castle, where are York, Berkeley, and Seymour, with some three hundred men. Ross and Willoughby, who have hastened from Ravenspurgh, arrive and vow their aid to Bolingbroke's cause.

Berkeley enters and begins to deliver a message to Bolingbroke under his title of Duke of Hereford. Bolingbroke cuts him short: he will answer only to the title of Lancaster, whose estates he has returned to assume as rightfully his. Berkeley apologizes and says that he comes from York, lord governor of the kingdom, to find out what it is that Bolingbroke seeks with an army during Richard's absence.

York now enters, and Bolingbroke kneels to his uncle. York demands not his knee but his "humble heart." He will not be addressed as uncle: "I am no traitor's uncle." How has his nephew dared return from exile without leave, and why this show of arms? Does he think the realm without a ruler? He, York, has power to act in the King's name. If he had his youth back, he would make his nephew feel some powerful correction. Bolingbroke replies that he was banished as Hereford, but has come back as Duke of Lancaster. Let his uncle be sympathetic, and stand in place of his late father, Gaunt, York's brother. Will York consent to see him condemned like some "wandering vagabond" when he is entitled to the privileges of a member of the royal family ("my rights and royalties")? Will he permit Bolingbroke's rightful possessions to be given away to Richard's pet spendthrifts? He himself is as justly Lancaster as Richard is King of England. Had York pre-deceased his son, Aumerle, and were Gaunt still alive, Gaunt would have acted like a father and hunted down Aumerle's enemies to the last extremity ("to the bay"). He himself has come to claim only what is his.

Northumberland, Ross and Willoughby second Bolingbroke's claims. York admits that Bolingbroke has been wronged, and that he did all he could in his behalf; but when it comes to taking up arms and choosing the means of rebellion to achieve justice, they are wrong to aid and abet his nephew. Northumberland asserts that Bolingbroke has sworn that he has come, not for rebellion, but only to claim his own; his friends have taken oath to help him.

York confesses to having no power to stop them; if he had he would force them to yield. Since he cannot, he will remain neutral. At any rate, let them accept the hospitality of the castle for the night. Bolingbroke accepts, but insists that York thence accompany them to Bristol Castle, where Bushy, Bagot and the other cancers ("caterpillars") of the kingdom are hiding. York says he may go with them, but must think it over; he has no desire to infringe the law of the land.

◆ *Commentary.* One reason for believing that Shakespeare was already planning to write *Henry IV, Part I* is that when (his own invention) he introduces Percy here, he makes him the youth that he is to be in the later play. Historically, Percy was two years Bolingbroke's senior.

In *Henry IV* (where Worcester, Percy's uncle, starts the rebellion of the Percy family), Henry Percy ("Hotspur") will have cause bitterly to remember Bolingbroke's promise, in this scene, of future rewards for the support of the Percies:

> *Why, what a candy deal of courtesy*
> *This fawning greyhound then did proffer me!*
> *Look, "when his infant fortune came to age,"*
> *And, "gentle Harry Percy," and "kind cousin"—*
> *O, the devil take such cozeners!*

(I, iii, 251 seq.)

The Duke of York here at first tries to be loyal to Richard, but his very words of reproof bespeak his impotence and failing years. Bolingbroke sounds reasonable enough, but his announced purposes, as will be revealed, are false. York soon is justifying himself to Northumberland and the others, and before their staunchness presently confesses his powerlessness. Bolingbroke's words on the inmates of Bristol Castle foreshadow his having ends larger than the recovery of his estates.

Though the concept of this scene derives from Holinshed, the matter of the dialogue is Shakespeare's own, including York's neutrality.

These are the relevant passages in Holinshed:

> The duke of Yorke, whome king Richard had left as governour of the realme in his absence, hearing that his nephue the duke of Lancaster was thus arrived, and had gathered an armie, he also assembled a puissant power of men of armes . . . but all was in vaine, for there was not a man that willinglie would thrust one arrow against the duke of Lancaster, or his partakers, or in anie wise offend him or his freends. The duke of Yorke therefore passing foorth towards Wales to meet the king, at his comming foorth of Ireland, was received into the castell of Berkelie, and there remained, till the comming thither of the duke of Lancaster (whom when he perceived that he was not able to resist) on the sundaie, after the feast of saint James, which as that yeare came about, fell upon the fridaie, he came foorth into the church that stood without the castell, and there communed with the duke of Lancaster.

Shakespeare has chosen a simpler and more dramatic locale for the interview.

SCENE 4. A camp in Wales: Salisbury and a Welsh Captain. The Captain tells Salisbury that since there has been no word of the King for ten days, he is disbanding his troops. Salisbury begs him to wait a little longer, for the King depends upon his Welsh supporters. The Captain replies that rumor has it that Richard is dead. Moreover, there have been terrifying portents of nature in the form of withered trees, meteors, a bloody moon—such as herald the fall of kings. The Welsh devoted to the King have fled, and he will run too. He goes out. Salisbury forsees nothing but disaster in store for Richard.

◆ *Commentary.* This scene in its details follows Holinshed fairly closely:

> In this yeere in a manner throughout all the realme of

England, old baie trees withered, and afterwards, contrarie to
all mens thinking, grew greene againe. . . .

There was a brute spred amongst them, that the king was
suerlie dead, which wrought such an impression, and evill dis-
position in the minds of the Welshmen and others, that for anie
persuasion which the earle of Salisburie might use, they would
not go foorth with him, till they saw the king: onelie they were
contented to staie fourteene daies to see if he should come or not;
but when he came not within that tearme, they would no longer
abide, but scaled and departed awaie; whereas if the king had
come before their breaking up, no doubt, they would have put
the duke of Hereford in adventure of a field.

Daniel's *Civil Wars* has the following passage:
Red fiery dragons in the aire doe flie,
And burning Meteors, poynted-streaming lights,
Bright starres in midst of day appeare in skie,
Prodigious monsters, gastly fearefull sights . . .

but such portents were commonplace in Elizabethan drama, as a
number of Shakespeare's plays evidence.

Act III

SCENE 1. Bristol, before the Castle: Bolingbroke, York, Northumberland, Ross, Percy, Willoughby; Bushy and Green prisoners.
Bolingbroke addresses the prisoners: since they are about to lose
their lives, he wishes the world to know the reason for their executions. They have completely misled Richard; they have separated
the King from his Queen's bed, causing her endless grief. It was
they who urged the King to misjudge Bolingbroke, and who are
responsible for the injuries done him. While he was bitterly eating
the bread of banishment, they were feeding upon his estates and
trying to eradicate all memory of him. Bushy says that death is more
welcome to him than Bolingbroke will prove to England; Green
prophecies that Bolingbroke will find them avenged when he goes
to Hell. They are led off to their executions. Bolingbroke asks York
to see that the queen is well treated, and to send her his compli-
ments.

◆ *Commentary.* Shakespeare has invented Bolingbroke's charges against Bushy and Green. His innuendo that they have led Richard into homosexual practices and separated him from his queen has, amazingly, been taken as fact by many commentators. Yet it is quite clear from the play that this was not at all Shakespeare's meaning. In the last act Richard says to Northumberland:

> *Bad men, you violate*
> *A twofold marriage, 'twixt my crown and me,*
> *And then betwixt me and my married wife . . .*
> *Part us, Northumberland . . .*
> *She came adorned hither like sweet May,* etc.
>
> V, i, 71 seq.

Earlier in the same scene the love between Richard and his Queen is made clear enough. Had Shakespeare meant what Bolingbroke falsely charges, he would have shown it to us in the play, and it nowhere so appears. The charges are to be read as part of Bolingbroke's unscrupulous methods. Part of the portrait is his pretended solicitude for the Queen, whose champion he pretends to be. At most, Richard's favorites flattered him and lived off his bounty.

This is the relevant passage in Holinshed:

> There were inclosed within the castell, . . . sir Henrie Greene, and sir John Bushie knights . . . ; they were taken and brought foorth bound as prisoners into the campe, before the duke of Lancaster. On the morrow next insuing, they were arraigned before the constable and marshall, and found guiltie of treason, for misgoverning the king and realme, and foorthwith had their heads smit off.

SCENE 2. The coast of Wales: Richard, the Bishop of Carlisle, Aumerle, and Soldiers. Richard weeps for joy that he stands again upon England's soil, and bids it reject the rebels who harm it with their "treacherous feet." When his foes stoop to pluck a flower may they find that behind it lurks a death-dealing adder! The Bishop vows that the King's men will remain faithful—yes, even should Heaven itself demand otherwise. Aumerle feels they have been too remiss in opposing Bolingbroke's power, but the King chides him: when the sun is hidden at night, then robbers and murderers appear to do their villainy; but when the sun reappears, they are stripped and exposed for what they are. So too will Boling-broke cringe before the returning sunlight of the King's presence again in England. For every man in Bolingbroke's pay, Richard has an angel defending him in Heaven.

Salisbury comes in, and is asked where his army lies. Salisbury replies that he can speak only discouragement ("discomfort") —the King is one day too late. Yesterday Richard could have had twelve thousand Welshmen fighting for him; today, having heard the rumor that the King was dead, they have either dispersed or gone to join Bolingbroke. Though paling at this news, Richard tries to spur his courage; after all, he is still King, and he can count on the loyalty of his uncle York.

Scroop enters with words indicating that he has only disasters to report. At once Richard cries: "Is my kingdom lost?" Glad that the King is prepared for the worst, Scroop tells him that even old men, women, and mere boys have taken up arms for Bolingbroke; he also informs Richard euphemistically that Bagot, Bushy, and Green have made their "peace" with the foe. Misunderstanding him, Richard breaks forth into vituperation against his old favorites for their treachery; each is worse than Judas. Scroop corrects him: he meant they had made their peace by surrendering their heads— as have "all of them at Bristol,"—for being Richard's friends. Aumerle asks where his father, York, is. The King interrupts: what matter where York may be? It is here that he makes his famous apostrophe: *For God's sake, let us sit upon the ground | And tell sad stories of the death of kings . . ."* He already feels the doom, visited upon so many monarchs, upon him too. The Bishop up-braids him for accepting defeat so readily: it is better to fight than to indulge this suicidal mood; Aumerle agrees, and Richard plucks up courage. Now Scroop delivers the heaviest blow of all: York has joined forces with Bolingbroke, and has surrendered all of the King's northern castles and southern gentlemen-in-arms.

Richard turns on Aumerle: what comfort has he to offer now? The King will only hate anyone who talks more of taking heart; he himself will go to Flint Castle (in Wales) , dismiss his army, and pine away. Aumerle tries to dissuade him, but Richard will not listen.

◆ *Commentary.* Since Holinshed locates Richard's arrival in Wales at "Barclowlie," Shakespeare follows suit; historically the locale was Harlech. Coleridge's remarks on this scene are interesting: "Shakespeare has carefully shown in him [Richard] an intense love of country, well knowing how that feeling would, in pure historic drama, redeem him in the hearts of the audience."

In Holinshed Richard hears of Bolingbroke's success while still in Ireland. Here he seems to have arrived with that knowledge, but with no precise information on the details.

It is to be noted that Richard's overwrought "But now the blood of twenty thousand men" etc. is written in the form of a sestet, and that Scroop's "Men judge by the complexion of the sky" as a quatrain—both characteristic of Shakespeare's early style.

We have seen Bushy and Green led to their executions in the preceding scene. Here it is announced that Bagot was killed with them too. Yet in the fourth act we find that Bagot is still alive; it will also be remembered that in II, ii, Bagot announced his intention of joining Richard in Ireland. Perhaps Shakespeare, who was sometimes careless of small details in the story, became confused here because of his source.

Having already shown the causes of Richard's overthrow in the earlier part of the play, Shakespeare now settles down to a revelation, in the rest of the drama, of the conflicts and self-examinations within his hero himself, as piece by piece Richard will have to surrender, as we already know he must, the little that is left to him. In the process, as Richard falls, degree by degree, he reveals himself as a highly expressive poet.

This is the relevant passage in Holinshed:

At length, about eighteene daies after that the king had sent from him the duke of Salisburie, he tooke the sea, togither with the dukes of Aumarle, Exeter, Surrie, and divers others of the nobilitie . . . They landed neere the castell of Barclowlie in Wales, about the feast of saint James the apostle, and staied a while in the same castell, being advertised of the great forces which the duke of Lancaster had got togither against him, wherewith he was marvellouslie amazed, knowing certeinlie that those which were thus in armes with the duke of Lancaster against him, would

rather die than give place, as well for the hate as feare which
they had conceived at him . . .

Richard departs from the castle and goes "towards Conwaie,"
because he expects to find Salisbury there:

He doubted not to revenge himselfe of his adversaries, and
so he passed with a good courage; but when he understood as he
went thus forward, that all the castels, even from the borders of
Scotland unto Bristow were delivered unto the duke of Lancaster,
and that likewise the nobles and commons, as well of the south
parts, as the north, were fullie bent to take part with the same
duke against him; and further, hearing how his trustie councellors
had lost their heads at Bristow, he became so greatlie discom-
forted, that sorrowfullie lamenting his miserable state, he utterlie
despaired of his own safetie, and calling his armies togither,
which was not small, licensed every man to depart to his home.
His souldiers being well bent to fight in his defense, besought
him to be of good cheere, promising with an oth to stand with
him against the duke, and all his partakers unto death: but this
could not incourage him at all, so that in the night next insuing,
he stole from his armie.

The invented episode of Richard's at first misapprehending
Scroop to mean that his favorites had gone over to the enemy,
serves to show how quick Richard is to be wounded, and how ready
he already is to surrender everything. When he learns that they have
been killed he has nothing to say about them. His grief is self-
centered.

SCENE 3.   Before Flint Castle (Wales) : Bolingbroke, York, Northumberland, and Attendants. Bolingbroke has just learned of
Richard's arrival in England and of the dispersal of the Welsh
troops. Northumberland speaks slightingly of the King as "Richard," and is reprimanded by Bolingbroke for not employing the
monarch's title: the conqueror implies his intended respect for the
King's position. York adds his own reproof: there was a time that
Northumberland would not have dared being so short in referring
to the King. But this does not altogether please Bolingbroke, who
bids his uncle York not go further than he should. Whereupon
York counters: let the victor not *take* more than he should!

Percy comes in to say that Flint Castle is manned against Bolingbroke, that the King, Aumerle, Salisbury, Carlisle, and Scroop are also within it. Bolingbroke commands that this message be delivered: Bolingbroke comes to lay before King Richard his arms and army on condition that his exile be repealed and his seized lands all restored; otherwise, Engand will be drenched in blood. If Richard will be fire, Bolingbroke will be water.

A trumpet is sounded for parley, and the King with his friends appears on the walls. York notes with admiration how much Richard looks like a monarch still. Richard addresses Northumberland: he had expected Northumberland to bend his knee in awe of majesty; what force has wrested kingship from Richard? God himself in mustering "armies of pestilence" in the King's behalf, and every kind of ill will be visited upon the rebels and their children. Let Northumberland tell Bolingbroke that every step the latter takes in England is an act of treason, and that he comes to open up the bloody sluices of war. Northumberland speaks Bolingbroke's message, assuring Richard that all his cousin wishes is what are his rights. Richard agrees at once to entertain all of Bolingbroke's demands. And having said as much, he asks of Aumerle whether it was not base to have so yielded. Aumerle approves of diplomatic behavior at this time, but Richard grieves at being so much reduced that he must rescind his enemy's banishment.

Seeing Northumberland returning from Bolingbroke's side, the King breaks forth into a speech which anticipates evils which have not been mentioned: What must he do now—submit to Bolingbroke —be deposed? If so, let it be so—he will retire to a monastery to pray or wait for an obscure grave. Aumerle is weeping at his cousin's plight, and Richard offers to match tears with him. Northumberland has only this to say: Bolingbroke awaits Richard in the lower court. Richard agrees, likening his coming down to the fall of Phaeton. He leaves the walls, and presently appears below.

Bolingbroke kneels to Richard, but the King mocks him for debasing his "princely knee." Does not Bolingbroke's ambition mount as high as to Richard's crown? Bolingbroke's reply is that he has come only for his own possessions. I am your own, too, Richard says bitterly. He sees his old uncle York weeping, and takes his hands. He promises to give Bolingbroke all he wishes to have, since force is the great persuader. He supposes that his cousin requires his return to London, and Bolingbroke does not deny it.

◆ *Commentary.* In the Elizabethan theatre, the walls of a castle or town were easily imagined when the actors appeared on the balcony above the stage. Thus Richard and his friends came out on this balcony, and the stage itself was understood to represent the plains before the castle.

In this scene we become even more aware of Richard's curious ability to suffer and at the same time see himself suffering, as though he were a spectator at a play which was depicting his own tragedy. Again he anticipates evil instead of withstanding it, and is prepared to surrender his crown before Bolingbroke has even asked for it. He seems almost in love with his own pitiable condition, and while Aumerle weeps in sincere sympathy for his plight, Richard's deliberately extending the drama into theatricalism by offering to match tears with him deprives him of dignity at the same time as it fascinates us with his character.

York's desperate attempt to maintain loyalty to Richard even though he has yielded to Bolingbroke's power is briefly but strikingly portrayed, as is Northumberland's coldness. Bolingbroke alone plays the perfect politician in his adroitness and, despite Richard's weakness, not giving voice to his ultimate goals. His strength is the more manifest in his being thus so courteous and self-controlled, while he is already ordering the King's movements.

Shakespeare has compressed the action as he found it in Holinshed, with admirable dramatic consequences. In the source, the King was proceeding to Conway, where Northumberland promised to bring him safely thence to Bolingbroke for a conference; en route, Richard was ambushed and carried to Flint Castle, while Bolingbroke was still at Chester. Now Bolingbroke led his army to Flint Castle, sent Northumberland on several missions to Richard, and then appeared himself before the King. Among the demands of Bolingbroke which Shakespeare has omitted is the condition that a Parliament be appointed that would wreak vengeance on Bolingbroke's enemies and avenge the murder of Gloucester.

It is interesting to note how Shakespeare has put to good use in this scene a passage that occurs much earlier in Holinshed, when King Richard has Gloucester arrested, as the monarch rode "into the base court, his trumpets sounding before him. The duke [Gloucester] herewith came downe into the base court."

These are the relevant passages in Holinshed:

> After this, the duke, with advise of his councell, sent the earle of Northumberland unto the king, accompanied with foure hundred lances, and a thousand archers, who coming to the castell of Flint, had it delivered unto him; and from thence he hasted foorth toward Conwaie. But before he approached neere the place, he left his power behind him, hid closelie in two ambushes . . .
>
> This doone, taking not past foure or five with him, he passed foorth, till he came before the towne, and then sending an herald to the king, requested a safe conduct from the king, . . . which the king granted, . . . and comming to the king, declared to him, that if it might please his grace to undertake, that there should be a parlement assembled, in the which iustice might be had, against such as were enimies to the common-wealth, and had procured the destruction of the duke of Glocester, and other noblemen, and herewith pardon the duke of Hereford of all things wherein he had offended him, the duke would be readie to come to him on his knees, to crave of him forgiveness, and as an humble subiect, to obeie him in all dutifull services. The king taking advise upon these offers, . . . upon the earles oth, . . . agreed to go with the earle to meete the duke, and hereupon taking their horsses, they rode foorth, but the earle rode before, . . . but comming to the place where he had left his people, he staied there with them.
>
> The king keeping on his waie, had not ridden past foure miles, when he came to the place where the ambushes were lodged, . . . There was no remedie: for the earle being there with his men, would not suffer him to returne . . . ; but being inclosed with the sea on the one side, and the rocks on the other, having his adversaries so neere at hand before him, he could not shift awaie by any meanes . . . And thus of force he was then constrained to go with the earle, who brought him to . . . Flint . . .
>
> King Richard being thus come unto the castell of Flint, on the mondaie, the eighteenth of August, and the duke of Hereford being still advertised from houre to houre by posts, . . . the

morrow following being tuesdaie, and the nineteenth of August, he came thither, & mustered his armie before the kings presence. . . .

The king that was walking aloft on the braies of the wals, to behold the comming of the duke a farre off, might see, that the archbishop and the other [Canterbury, Aumerle, Worcester, and others] were come, and (as he tooke it) to talke with him: whereupon he foorthwith came downe unto them, and beholding that they did their due reverence to him on their knees, he toooke them up . . .

Then the earle of Northumberland passing foorth of the castell to the duke, talked with him a while in sight of the king, being againe got up to the walles, to take better view of the armie . . . After he [Richard] had dined, the duke came downe to the castell himselfe, and entred the same all armed, . . . and being within the first gate, he staied there, till the king came foorth of the inner part of the castell unto him. . . .

Foorthwith as the duke got sight of the king, he shewed a reverend dutie as became him, in bowing his knee, and comming forward, did so likewise the second and third time, till the king tooke him by the hand, and lift him up, saieing; Deere cousine, ye are welcome. The duke humblie thanking him said; My sovereigne lord and king, the cause of my comming at this present, is . . . to have againe restitution of my person, my lands and heritage, through your favourable licence. The king herunto answered; Deere cousine, I am readie to accomplish your will, so that ye may inioy all that is yours, without exception.

Meeting thus togither, they came foorth of the castell, . . . and after they had dronke, they mounted on horssebacke. . . .

This scene is a fine example of Shakespeare's ability to follow a source, and yet alter it with imaginative power that brings dull fact into pulsing life.

SCENE 4. The Duke of York's Garden: the Queen and Two Ladies. The Queen asks what sport they can play to pass the weary hours. One lady suggests the game of bowls, but the Queen protests that that will be too full of impediments ("rubs"); as it is her fortune is all too crooked ("against the bias"—the bias was the leaden weight in the ball). She will not dance either because of her grief, nor will she hear tales of joy or sorrow; joy will only remind her of her woe, and of sorrow she has enough. A Gardener and two servants enter, and the ladies retire to the shade of the trees to listen to their talk.

The Gardener gives his orders to his assistants, but one of them asks why they should trouble to keep order in a garden when the whole country is choked with weeds. The Gardener replies that Bolingbroke has plucked up by the roots the flourishing weeds of state, Wiltshire, Bushy, and Green. What a pity that the "wasteful King" did not do with his land as they are doing with their garden, lopping away what was needful to cut in order to give the boughs life; had he done so he might still have kept his crown. The Gardener is sure that Richard will be deposed.

The Queen steps forth and chides him for his prophecy. He answers that it gives him no joy to tell the news: but Richard is in Bolingbroke's power, and all the English nobility is for Bolingbroke. Overwhelmed to be the last to hear the dire tidings, the Queen decides to hasten to London.

The ladies go out. The Gardener pities the Queen, and will plant some rue on the spot where she let fall a tear.

◆ *Commentary.* This scene is Shakespeare's invention.

When the ladies retire to the shade of the trees, on the Elizabethan stage the actors would simply have moved to the inner stage, the regular place for "overhearing."

It is Shakespeare's habit in his tragedies to introduce some character who represents the human norm, against whom the shortcomings of the hero and other characters may be measured—e.g., Horatio in *Hamlet,* Kent in *Lear,* Benvolio in *Romeo and Juliet.* In this case that person is the Gardener. Though of humble station, his sanity throws into relief the weaknesses of Richard and the ambitions of Bolingbroke. It is a scene beautifully conceived and executed.

Act IV

SCENE 1. London: a session of Parliament, with Bolingbroke, Aumerle, Northumberland, Percy, Fitzwater, Surrey, the Bishop of

Carlisle, the Abbot of Westminster, Herald, Officers, and Lords. Bagot is brought in, and questioned by Bolingbroke concerning the murder of Gloucester. Bagot accuses Aumerle of complicity, and quotes him as saying that he would rather refuse a hundred thousand crowns than see Bolingbroke's exile revoked, and that Bolingbroke's death would be a blessing for England.

Aumerle, charging Bagot with being a liar, throws down his gage in challenge to his accuser. Bolingbroke orders Bagot not to pick it up. Fitzwater now throws down his gage, asserting that he heard Aumerle boast of being the cause of Gloucester's death. Aumerle denies this charge too. Percy backs Fitzwater and throws down his gage, and is joined by another lord. Aumerle is ready to fight them all.

Surrey interrupts. He was present on the occasion of which Fitzwater has spoken, and he denounces Fitzwater as a liar—and challenges him to fight. Fitzwater maintains his charges, and adds that he heard banished Mowbray (Norfolk) say that Aumerle sent two of his men to kill Gloucester. Aumerle accepts each and every one of these challenges to a fight.

Bolingbroke declares that their differences will have to await the return of Mowbray. Although Bolingbroke's enemy, he shall be recalled from exile. But the Bishop of Carlisle tells them that Mowbray, after fighting in Jerusalem, died at Venice. Bolingbroke, after a prayer for Mowbray's soul, dismisses the quarrels over Aumerle for the present.

York enters with the news that Richard has yielded up his sceptre and allots it to Bolingbroke. Bolingbroke is ready to ascend the throne, but is stopped by the Bishop. Everyone present, he says, is still Richard's subject, and Bolingbroke is acting the part of a traitor if he claims the crown. Should the Parliament go along with Bolingbroke's ambition, the Bishop foresees ages of civil bloodshed in England. Whereupon, Northumberland arrests the Bishop for treason.

Bolingbroke has Richard sent for, that he may surrender his crown publicly. York goes to bring him. While waiting, Bolingbroke makes clear in an aside ("Little are we beholding to your love . . .") that he means to avenge himself on Richard's friends.

York re-enters with Richard. Richard observes that he has not yet learned how to flatter and bow. Were not all these men once his?

Did they not all once hail him? They are so many Judases; yet Jesus found only one out of twelve a traitor; he himself has found loyalty in not one out of twelve thousand. Why is he sent for?

To give up the crown which he himself has offered to do, York answers. Richard takes the crown from his attendant, and urges Bolingbroke to take hold of half of it. Bolingbroke wrily says that he thought Richard wished to abdicate. In a long speech, resigning everything, Richard lets go of the crown and hails Bolingbroke as King Henry. What else, he demands, is expected of him?

Northumberland hands him a paper listing the "crimes" committed by Richard and his followers against the country and its prosperity. Let Richard confess them, so that the world may know that he is being deposed with reason. Richard begs for some pity. He is weeping so bitterly that he cannot read the paper. He wishes he were a king of snow that he might melt before the sun of Bolingbroke. He requests a mirror that he may see himself in this new role of being nothing. Northumberland tries to press the list of indictments upon him, but Bolingbroke bids him desist.

The mirror is brought and Richard is surprised to find no deep wrinkles in his face, despite all he has suffered, and dashes the mirror to pieces. He asks one favor of Bolingbroke: the leave to go anywhere out of the usurper's sight. Bolingbroke orders him taken to the Tower. Richard is led out. Bolingbroke announces his coronation for next Wednesday.

The Abbot of Westminister, the Bishop of Carlisle, and Aumerle, who are left on the stage as the others leave, decide to conspire against this usurpation.

◆ *Commentary.* For this highly dramatic scene Shakespeare has again compressed the events as he found them in Holinshed. On September 29, Richard abdicated before certain designated persons and signed the documents surrendering the crown; on September 30, these persons reported to Parliament, and with Parliament's consent Bolingbroke took the throne; on October 16, before Parliament, Bagot made the accusations against Aumerle; on October 22, the Bishop objected to Parliament's decision to pass sentence on Richard; on October 27, the new King promised to have Mowbray's exile revoked in order to clear up the charges made against Aumerle and to act upon them; some months later at the house of the Abbot of Westminster a plot was hatched against King Henry. It will be seen that, for dramatic effectiveness, Shakespeare has also rearranged these events and altered details.

Shakespeare having previously absent-mindedly killed off Bagot, as has been observed, retains him alive here, and in the disgusting role of a traitor to Richard.

Stripped already of all real power, Richard must now pay the price for his earlier rashness and misrule, and we can only await his loss of all he holds, piece by piece. There is nothing he can do. He has nothing supporting him. With his end inevitable, he begins to behave like an actor witnessing his own downfall. He toys with emotions and words, finding a miserable sort of comfort in tasting his sorrow before others. His pathetic play-acting brings forth no commiseration from his foes: Bolingbroke acts swiftly, coldly, and almost silently, and makes at best a stony audience, untouched by his wrongs to Richard.

Shakespeare has ignored chronology by making it appear that Gloucester was murdered during Bolingbroke's exile. Actually, Gloucester was killed before that began, as the first act of this play itself indicates. As for Mowbray's death, it is of course possible that we are to think that Bolingbroke had already heard of it when he promised to end Mowbray's banishment. It would not be inconsistent with his calculating efficiency, and ability to use everything that can advantage him. What he wanted was to cast suspicion upon Aumerle by going into the matter of Gloucester's death; having achieved his end, he does not even bother bringing Aumerle to trial.

Richard in his folly simply gives up his one chance to make decent provision for himself. Bolingbroke clearly has exposed himself as obliged to grant Richard the "one boon" he requests, and asks Richard to name it. Instead of taking measures for his security, in the presence of Parliament, all he asks is the privilege of being where he never has to see any of them again. He throws away his life for the sake of an effective gesture.

These are the relative passages in Holinshed:

> The next day after his comming to London, the king from Westminster was had to the Tower, and there committed to safe custodie. Manie evill disposed persons, assembling themselves togither in great numbers, intended to have met with him, and

to have taken him from such as had the conveieng of him, that they might have slaine him. But the mayor and aldermen gathered to them the worshipfull commoners and grave citizens, by whose policie, and not without much adoo, the other were revoked from their evill purpose . . .

After this was a parlement called by the duke of Lancaster, using the name of king Richard in the writs directed foorth to the lords, and other states for their summons. This parlement began the thirteenth daie of September, in the which manie heinous points of misgovernance and iniurious dealings in the administration of his kinglie office, were laid to the charge of this noble prince king Richard, the which (to the end the commons might be persuaded, that he was an unprofitable prince to the common-wealth, and worthie to be deposed) were ingrossed up in 33 solemne articles, heinous to the eares of all men, and to some almost incredible . . .

Then for so much as these articles, and other heinous and detestable accusations were laid against him in open parlement, it was thought by the most part, that he was worthie to be deposed from all kinglie honor, and princelie governement: and . . . diverse of the kings servants, which by licence had accesse to his person, comforted him . . . , exhorting him to regard his health, and save his life.

And first, they advised him willinglie to suffer himselfe to be deposed, and to resigne his right of his owne accord, so that the duke of Lancaster might without murther or battell obteine the scepter and diademe, after which . . . he gaped: by meane whereof they thought he might be in perfect assurance of his life long to continue . . . Notwithstanding, the king being now in the hands of his enemies, and utterlie despairing of all comfort, was easilie persuaded to renounce his crowne and princelie preheminence, so that in hope of life onelie, he agreed to all things that were of him demanded. And so . . . he renounced and voluntarilie was deposed from his roiall crowne and kinglie dignitie, the mondaie being the nine and twentith daie of September, and feast of S. Michaell the archangell, in the yeare of our lord *1399,* and in the three and twentith yeare of his reigne . . .

[There follows "a copie of the instrument touching the declaration of the commissioners sent from the states in parlement, unto king Richard." These commissioners, who included in their number York, Northumberland, and the Abbot of Westminster, between eight and nine in the morning of September 29 appeared at the Tower] in the cheefe chamber of the kings lodging, within the said place of the Tower, where was rehearsed unto the king by . . . Northumberland [that Richard had promised Northumberland] . . . that he for insufficiencie which he knew himselfe to be of, to occupie so great a charge, as to governe the realme of England, he would gladlie leave of and renounce his right and title . . . unto Henrie duke of Hereford . . . To the which rehearsall, the king in our said presences answered benignlie and said, that such promise he made, and so to do the same he was at that houre in full purpose to performe and fulfill; saving that he desired first to have personall speach with the said duke . . .

[Bolingbroke, Canterbury and the commissioners came to the Tower to see Richard.]

Where after due obeisance doone by them unto the king, he familiarlie and with a glad countenance . . . talked with the said archbishop and duke in good season: . . . the king with glad countenance in presence of us and the other above rehearsed, said openlie that he was readie to renounce and resigne all his kinglie maiestie in maner and forme as he before had promised. . . .

[Richard himself read aloud the scroll of abdication, which absolved all men] from their oth of fealtie . . . unto me . . . And also I resigne all my kinglie dignitie, maiestie and crowne, . . . except the lands and possessions for me and mine obits purchased and bought. And I renounce . . . the rule and governance of the same kingdome . . .

And also I renounce the name, worship, and regaltie and kinglie highnesse, clearlie, freelie, singularlie and wholie, in the most best maner and forme that I may, and with deed and word I leave off and resigne them, and go from them for evermore . . . And for more record of the same, here openlie I subscribe and signe this present resignation with mine owne hand.

Now foorthwith in our presences and others, he subscribed the same, saeing . . . he would that the duke of Lancaster there present should be his successour, and king after him. And in token hereof, he tooke a ring of gold from his finger being his signet, and put it upon the said dukes finger . . . All this doone everie man tooke their leave and returned to their owne . . .

[On the next day, Tuesday, September 30, Richard's scroll of abdication was exhibited to Parliament. The abdication was confirmed by the body there met, as well as by the commons.] After this, it was then declared, that notwithstanding the foresaid renouncing, . . . it were necessarie in avoiding of all suspicions and surmises of evill disposed persons, to have in writing and registred the manifold crimes and defaults before doone by king Richard, to the end that they might first be openlie declared to the people, and after to remaine of record amongst other of the kings records for ever . . .

[Now Bolingbroke formally claimed the throne as rightfully his; the Commons agreed, and the date for the coronation was set for October 13.] Thus was king Richard deprived of all kinglie honour and princelie dignitie, by reason he was so given to follow evill counsell, and used such inconvenient waies and meanes, through insolent misgovernance, and youthfull outrage. . . . He reigned two and twentie yeares, three moneths and eight daies. He delivered to king Henrie now that he was thus deposed, all the goods that he had, to the summe of three hundred thousand pound in coine, besides plate and iewels, as a pledge and satisfaction of the iniuries by him committed and doone, in hope to be in more suertie of life . . . but whatsoever was promised, he was deceived therein. For shortlie after his resignation, he was conveied to the castell of Leeds in Kent, & from thence to Pomfret, where he departed out of this miserable life (as after you shall heare.) He was seemlie of shape and favor, & of nature good inough, if the wickednesse & naughtie demeanor of such as were about him had not altered it.

. . . He was prodgall, ambitious, and much given to the pleasure of the bodie. He . . . mainteined the most plentifull house that ever any king in England did either before his time or since. For there resorted dailie to his court above ten thousand persons that had meat and drinke allowed them. In his kitchen there were three servitors . . . Of ladies, chamberers, and launderers, there were above three hundred at the least. And in gorgious and costlie apparell they exceeded all measure, not one of them that kept within the bounds of his degree. Yeomen and groomes were clothed in silkes. . . .

Furthermore, there reigned abundantlie the filthie sinne of leacherie and fornication, with abhominable adulterie, speciallie in the king, but most cheefelie in the prelacie, whereby the whole realme by such their evill example, was so infected, that the wrath of God was dailie provoked. . . .

But . . . he was a prince the most unthankfullie used of his subjects, of any one of whom ye shall lightlie read . . . [With all Richard's dissoluteness] in no kings daies were the commons in greater wealth . . . neither in any other time were the nobles and gentlemen more cherished, nor churchmen less wronged. But such was their ingratitude towards their bountiful and loving sovereigne. . . .

Although his [the Duke of Gloucester's] nephue the duke of Hereford tooke upon him to revenge his death, yet wanted he moderation and loyaltie in his dooings. . . .

Much adoo there was in this parlement [when it met on October 16, 1399], speciallie about them that were thought to be guiltie of the duke of Glocester's death. . . . Sir John Bagot knight then prisoner in the Tower, disclosed manie secrets, unto the which he was privie; and . . . a bill was read . . . which he made, conteining certeine evill practises of king Richard; and further what great affection the same king bare to the duke of Aumarle, insomuch that he heard him say, that if he should renounce the governement of the kingdome, he wished to leave it to the said duke . . . ; for though he could like better of the duke of Hereford, yet he said that he knew if he were once king, he would prove an extreame enimie and cruell tyrant to the church. . . . There was also conteined in the same bill, what secret malice king Richard had conceived against the duke of Hereford being in exile. . . . There was conteined in the said bill, that Bagot had heard the duke of Aumarle say, that he had rather than twentie thousand pounds that the duke of Hereford were dead . . . for the trouble and mischeefe that he was like to procure within the realme.

[After Bagot was questioned] . . . the lord Fitzwater rose up, and said . . . that he [Aumerle] was the verie cause of his [the Duke of Gloucester's] death, and so he appealed him of treason, offering by throwing downe his hood as a gage to prove it with his bodie. There were twentie other lords also that threw downe their hoods, as pledges to prove the like matter against the duke of Aumarle. . . .

[The Commons requested on the following Wednesday] that sith king Richard had resigned, and was lawfullie deposed from his roiall dignitie, he might have judgement decreed against him, . . . and that the causes of his deposing might be published through the realme for satisfieng of the people: which demand was granted. Whereupon the bishop of Carleill, a man both learned, wise, and stout of stomach, boldlie shewed foorth his opinion concerning that demand: affirming that there was none amongst them woorthie or meet to give judgement upon so noble a prince as king Richard was. . . . Said he there is not so ranke a traitor, nor so errant a theef, nor yet so cruell a murtherer . . . deteined in prison for his offense, but he shall be brought before the justice to hear his judgement; and will ye proceed to the judgement of an anointed king, hearing neither his answer nor excuse? I say, that the duke of Lancaster whom ye call king, hath more trespassed to K. Richard & his realme, than king Richard hath doone either to him, or us . . . [When the Bishop had finished his speech] he was attached by the earle marshall, and committed to ward in the abbeie of saint albons.

But now to speake of the conspiracie, which was contrived by the abbat of Westminster as cheefe instrument. [He had heard Hereford say, when very young, that the churchmen had too much, and feared the new king would act to impoverish the Church.] . . . The abbat after he had felt the minds of sundrie of them [certain lords of the realm], called to his house on a day in the terme time, all such lords & other persons which he either knew or thought to be as affectioned to king Richard. . . .

. . . They sat downe in councell, and after much talke & conference had about the bringing of their purpose to passe concerning the destruction of king Henrie . . .

Act V

SCENE 1. A street in London leading to the Tower: The Queen and her ladies. The Queen remarks that the King will pass this way en route to the Tower, erected [according to legend] by Julius Caesar for evil purposes ("ill-erected"). Richard comes in under guard, and the Queen seeing how wasted he looks asks why ugly-faced ("hard-favoured") grief should lodge in him, a beauteous inn, while Bolingbroke, a common alehouse, is triumphing. He tries to comfort her by sounding resigned. He has become a sworn brother to grim Necessity. He bids her escape to some convent in France. She is desolate to find that Bolingbroke has stolen not only her husband's crown but his courage as well. He urges her to think of him as already dead, and hereafter on winter nights to tell her hearers his sad story, and send them "weeping to their beds."

Northumberland comes in with others and bluntly informs Richard that Bolingbroke has changed his mind, and that Richard is to go to Pomfret, not to the Tower; the Queen is also ordered to leave at once for France.

Richard prophesies that though Northumberland has been Bolingbroke's ladder, the time will come when he, having learned how to displant rightful kings, will work, through greed, to displant the new king too. Northumberland brusquely waves this aside, and tells Richard to hurry off to Pomfret.

There follows an affecting scene of parting between Richard and his Queen. She asks that either he be allowed to go with her to France or she be permitted to accompany him to Pomfret. Northumberland listens like a stone. Richard and his wife each goes his own way.

◆ *Commentary.* Historically, the King and Queen never met again after Richard had left for Ireland. In Daniel's *Civil Wars* there is a final meeting between the two, but it is totally different from Shakespeare's scene. In Daniel the Queen sees Richard from a window and then contrives a way to visit him in prison, where they are both speechless from sorrow.

The dialogue which Shakespeare has written for this scene should put beyond all discussion the deep affection between Queen and King, and reduce to absurdity the insistence of so many commentators that we are to understand Richard's partiality for his favorites as implying homosexual attachments. Richard speaks of his wife as having come to him from France adorned like sweet May; she speaks of him as her fair rose. Their parting has been most touchingly portrayed.

SCENE 2.   The Duke of York's house in London: York and his Duchess. The Duchess asks her husband to recount what happened between their two relatives ("cousins"), Richard and Bolingbroke. From windows the populace threw dust and rubbish at Richard as he was led through the streets, while they cried out "God save thee, Bolingbroke." Bolingbroke, on horseback, bowed graciously on all sides to his well-wishers. Richard, his face warring between smiles and tears at these insults, bore it all silently.

York's son, Aumerle, enters. He has been deprived of that title and now must be known by his other title as Earl of Rutland; he has also been forced to use his father, York, as a pledge of his loyalty to King Henry. The Duchess asks who are the new favorites ("violets") at court; Aumerle does not know or care. They speak of the jousts to be held. York sees a document sticking out of his son's jacket, insists upon examining it, and when Aumerle refuses, plucks it away himself. He reads it and sees that it contains treasonable matter, and calls at once for his horse. He will denounce the traitor, even though he is his own son. The Duchess upbraids her husband: Aumerle is their only son, and she is too old to bear another. York cries out: does she realize that according to the document a dozen men have taken an oath to kill Henry at Oxford? The Duchess begs that they keep Aumerle at home—that should satisfy York. He, however, in a rage promises to betray his son to King Henry. His wife pleads for Aumerle in vain, and York dashes out to reveal all to the King. The Duchess bids Aumerle follow him and get to Henry before his father, and beg to be forgiven before his father can speak what he knows. She will follow too and never cease until Henry pardons Aumerle.

◆ *Commentary.* Historically, the Duchess was not Aumerle's mother, as she is here, but his step-mother, the second wife of York.

It is rather astonishing to find York, who was so feeble in acting as Richard's representative, feeling such extravagant rage against his own son, and going so far as to be the agent of the younger man's death. The ruling emotion in York seems to be loyalty to the

crown, whoever the monarch at the moment. Remembering the
Divine Right of Kings, we must not forget that his attitude would
seem far more conventional to an Elizabethan audience than we are
able now to imagine it as having been.

This is the relevant passage in Holinshed:

> [At the Abbot of Westminster's meeting of conspirators, it
> was agreed] . . . that they should take upon them a solemne
> justs . . . at Oxford, to the which triumph K. Henrie should be
> desired, & . . . he suddenlie should be slaine and destroied, and
> so by that means king Richard, who as yet lived, might be
> restored to libertie. . . . They sware on the holie evangelists to
> be true and secret to each other. . . .
>
> [The] earle of Rutland departing from Westminster to see
> his father the duke of Yorke, as he sat at dinner, had his counter-
> pane of the indenture of the confederacie in his bosome.
>
> The father espieng it, would needs see what it was: and
> though the sonne humblie denied to shew it, the father being
> more earnest to see it, by force tooke it out of his bosome; and
> perceiving the contents thereof, in a great rage caused his horsses
> to be sadled out of hand, and spitefullie reprooving his sonne of
> treason, . . . he incontinentlie mounted on horssebacke to ride
> towards Windsore to the king, to declare unto him the malicious
> intent of his complices. The earle of Rutland seeing in what
> danger he stood, tooke his horsse, and rode another waie to
> Windsore in poste, so that he got thither before his father.

It is characteristic of Shakespeare that he should have made the
Duchess, whom he already equipped with true femininity and
motherliness, responsible for Aumerle's following his father to the
King.

SCENE 3.   Windsor Castle: Bolingbroke, Percy, and other Lords.

Bolingbroke speaks of his son Henry (the future Henry V).
The boy is leading the life of a profligate, and it is three months
since his father has even seen him. He asks his lords to seek him
out in low dives, where he keeps company with thieves and the
worst of ragamuffins. Percy reports that when he met the Prince
two days ago and told him about the solemnities to be held at
Oxford, the youth replied that he would wear a whore's glove as
his favor at the tournament. Bolingbroke hopes that his son will
mend with the years.

Aumerle comes in distraught, is granted private audience with Bolingbroke, falls to his knees and asks for pardon before he speaks out. Bolingbroke promises to forgive him, whatever his crime. Aumerle begs permission to lock the door, and is granted that. At once York appears at the door and cries to be allowed to enter, crying out to Bolingbroke to have care for Aumerle is a traitor. York insists upon being admitted or else he will break the door down. He is admitted, and shows Bolingbroke the document outlining the plot against the new king. Aumerle reminds Bolingbroke of his promise to pardon him; York cries out that Aumerle is thoroughly guilty and now repents out of fear, not love for the king. He urges Bolingbroke to punish Aumerle. Bolingbroke is minded to forgive the son of so loyal a father, but York insists that his son deserves to die.

The Duchess of York is at the door, demands admittance, and pleads with Bolingbroke not to listen to York. She kneels and begs for Aumerle's pardon. York kneels and begs for Aumerle's punishment. She prevails and Aumerle is pardoned. But all the other conspirators are to be condemned to death.

◆ *Commentary.* The reference to Bolingbroke's son has, of course, nothing to do with the business of this play. But it would seem to indicate that Shakespeare had already determined some day to write the *Henry IV* plays in which the Prince figures so prominently, and this little passage is a kind of sketch in advance of the character young Henry is to exhibit at the beginning of those histories. Actually, young Henry was *quite* young indeed at this time—only twelve years of age, and hardly capable of having the associates he is described as frequenting. (*Unthrifty* means *profligate*, *wanton* means *spoiled child*, *passengers* are *passers-by*, and *companions* is a term of contempt.)

York's fervent desire to have his son executed for treason is rather hard to accept; indeed, there is something a little absurd in the passage where York, his Duchess, and son all kneel imploring death for Aumerle on the one hand, and pardon on the other. The whole scene is marred by an excess of rhyme in Shakespeare's earliest manner (see lines 70-73; 87-146), and too much artifice of language ill-suiting the serious business of the scenario.

The pertinent passages in Holinshed follow:

The earle of Rutland [Aumerle] . . . got thither [Windsor] before his father, and when he was alighted at the castell gate, he caused the gates to be shut. . . . When he came before the kings presence he kneeled downe on his knees, beseeching him of mercie and forgivenesse, and declaring the whole matter unto him in order as everie thing had passed, obteined pardon. Therewith came his father, and being let in, delivered the indenture which he had taken from his sonne, unto the king, who thereby perceiving his sonnes words to be true, changed his purpose for his going to Oxenford . . .

It will be seen that, for dramatic reasons, Shakespeare has York come in before Aumerle has the chance to confess his guilt.

SCENE 4.   Another room in Windsor Castle: Exton and a Servant. Exton has heard Bolingbroke say twice: "Will no friend rid me of this living fear?" and observed that the new king was looking at him significantly as he said it. Exton understands that this "living fear" is Richard. Exton is resolved to prove himself the friend that will rid Bolingbroke of this fear.

◆ *Commentary.*   This is the passage in Holinshed:

One writer . . . saith, that king Henrie, sitting on a daie at his table, sore sighing, said: Have I no faithfull friend which will deliver me of him, whose life will be my death, and whose death will be the preservation of my life? This saeing was much noted of them which were present, and especiallie of one called sir Piers of Exton.

SCENE 5.   Pomfret Castle, a ward room: King Richard. Richard soliloquizes on his lot in prison. His thoughts "people" his cell. He sees himself playing many roles, all of them unhappy ones. Sometimes when he feels a king, he wishes himself a beggar. And a beggar he is, and so he wishes he were truly king again. Then when he feels like a king again, he is dethroned by Bolingbroke anew. Suddenly music is heard, and that sets him off upon a new flood of images. When he was king he wasted time, and now Time wastes him.

A groom of the stable enters, having come to look upon his old master's face; the groom's heart grieved when he saw Bolingbroke astride Richard's old horse. As the keeper comes in with a dish, the groom departs sadly. Richard refuses to eat of the dish until the keeper has tasted of it first; but that the keeper dare not do, having been commanded by Exton not to touch it. In anger Richard strikes the keeper, who calls for help.

Exton comes in with armed servants. Richard seizes an axe from one of them and kills him, and then kills another. Here Exton strikes Richard down. Richard curses him as he dies. Exton, admiring Richard's pluck, is not so sure that he did well in murdering Richard. He will bring Richard's body to King Henry.

◆ *Commentary.* Richard's soliloquy shows him still unable to face reality; he prefers to dally with ideas rather than encounter his danger. The groom's visit is touching. Richard's sudden violence with the keeper and then the armed servants, though we have been shown nothing to prepare us for such conduct on his part, reminds us that he has been a warrior-king. His own end is made sudden and violent by Shakespeare, perhaps too sudden to allow us time to be deeply affected. In comparison, the sufferings and death of Edward II in Marlowe's play are much more moving. Exton's change of heart also seems too immediate to be acceptable.

This is the relevant passage in Holinshed:

[Exton came to Pomfret with eight armed men, bidding the squire who served Richard] to doo so no more, saeing; Let him eat now, for he shall not long eat. King Richard sat downe to dinner, and was served without courtesie or assaie, whereupon much marvelling at the sudden change, he demanded of the esquier whie he did not his dutie; Sir (said he) I am otherwise commanded by Sir Piers of Exton, which is newlie come from K. Henrie. When king Richard heard that word, he tooke the kerving knife in his hand, and strake the esquier on the head, saeing The divell take Henrie of Lancaster and thee togither. And with that word, sir Piers entred the chamber, well armed, with eight tall men likewise armed, everie of them having a bill in his hand.

King Richard perceiving this, put the table from him, & steping to the formost man, wrung the bill out of his hands, & so valiantlie defended himselfe, that he slue foure of those that thus came to assaile him. Sir Piers being halfe dismaied herewith, lept into the chaire where king Richard was woont to sit, while the other foure persons fought with him, and chased him about the chamber . . . comming by the chaire, where sir Pier stood, he was felled with a stroke of a pollax which sir Piers gave him upon the head, and therewith rid him out of life . . . It is said, that sir Piers of Exton, after he had thus slaine him, wept right bitterlie, as one striken with the pricke of a giltie conscience.

It will be noted that, to avoid melodramtic effect, Shakespeare has Richard kill two men instead of four.

SCENE 6. Windsor Castle: Bolingbroke, York, other Lords and Attendants. There is news that the conspirators have burned the town of Cicester [Cirencester]. Northumberland enters with the tidings that the heads of the rebel Oxford, Blunt, Salisbury, and Kent have been sent by him to London. (The Folio edition of this play corrects the line to read Spencer instead of Oxford.) Fitzwater comes in with news of further execution of rebel leaders. Percy enters with the Bishop of Carlisle; the conspirator Abbot of Westminster is dead but Carlisle awaits Henry's sentence. Henry grants Carlisle his life but orders him to find some "secret place" to end his days.

Exton and his followers come in, bearing a coffin. He announces that he has brought the corpse of Henry's greatest enemy, Richard. Instead of thanking him, Henry upbraids Exton for performing a deed which will cause slander to Bolingbroke's reign. Exton protests that it was Henry who gave him the incentive to murder Richard. Henry replies that though he wished Richard dead he hates his assassin. Now that Richard is dead he loves him. Exton's reward must be only a guilty conscience, and he is banished by the King. Henry declares that his soul is full of woe, that he will wear mourning for Richard. He will make a voyage to Jerusalem to wash away the guilt of Richard's death.

◆ *Commentary.* The reports of the quelling of the rebellion perhaps follow one another too rapidly to have any dramatic effect. Bolingbroke's sorrow over Richard's death, Shakespeare's invention, can only be interpreted as another piece of his characteristic hypocrisy. Holinshed speaks of Richard's corpse being brought to the Tower of London, then to the city, and thence to St. Paul's Cathedral, where it lay three days. King Henry attended a requiem mass for the murdered king at Westminster. But it was Shakespeare's invention to have Exton bring the corpse into Henry's presence.

(Henry's son, King Henry V, later removed Richard's body with that of his queen to Westminster.)

It must be admitted that this scene as written is a weak one with which to terminate the play.

Criticisms of *Richard II*

Samuel Taylor Coleridge, *Notes on Shakespeare* (ca. 1812).

From the length of the speeches, and the circumstance that, with one exception, the events are all historical, and presented in their results, not produced by acts seen by, or taking place before, the audience, this tragedy is ill suited to our present large theatres. But in itself, and for the closet, I feel no hesitation in placing it as the first and most admirable of all Shakspeare's purely historical plays . . . The spirit of patriotic reminiscence is the all-permeating soul of this noble work. It is, perhaps, the most purely historical of Shakspeare's dramas. There are not in it, as in the others, characters introduced merely for the purpose of giving a greater individuality and realness, as in the comic parts of Henry IV, by presenting, as it were, our very selves . . .

It certainly seems that Shakspeare's historic dramas produced a very deep effect on the minds of the English people . . . Marl-borough, we know, was not ashamed to confess that his principal acquaintance with English history was derived from them; and I believe that a large part of the information as to our old names and achievements even now abroad is due, directly or indirectly, to Shakspeare.

Admirable is the judgment with which Shakspeare always in the first scenes prepares, yet how naturally, and with what conceal-ment of art, for the catastrophe. Observe how he presents the germ of all the after events in Richard's insincerity, partiality, arbitrari-ness, and favoritism, and in the proud, tempestuous, temperament of his barons. In the very beginning, also, is displayed that feature in Richard's character, which is never forgotten throughout the play—his attention to decorum, and high feeling of the kingly dignity.

William Hazlitt, *The Characters of Shakspear's Plays* (1817).

In *Richard II* the weakness of the king leaves us leisure to take a greater interest in the misfortunes of the man. After the first act, in which the arbitrariness of his behaviour only proves his want of resolution, we see him staggering under the unlooked-for blows of fortune, bewailing his loss of kingly power, not preventing it, sinking under the aspiring genius of Bolingbroke, his authority trampled on, his hopes failing him, and his pride crushed and broken down under insults and injuries, which his own misconduct had provoked, but which he has not courage or manliness to resent. The change of tone and behaviour in the two competitors for the throne according to their change of fortune, from the capricious sentence of banishment passed by Richard upon Bolingbroke, the suppliant offers and modest pretensions of the latter on his return, to the high and haughty tone with which he accepts Richard's resignation of the crown after the loss of all his power, the use which he makes of the deposed king to grace his triumphal progress through the streets of London, and the final intimation of his wish for his death . . . is marked throughout with complete effect and without the slightest appearance of effort. The steps by which Bolingbroke mounts the throne are those by which Richard sinks into the grave. We feel neither respect nor love for the deposed monarch; for he is as wanting in energy as in principle; but we pity him, for he pities himself. His heart is by no means hardened against himself, but bleeds afresh at every new stroke of mischance, and his sensibility, absorbed in his own person, and unused to misfortune, is not only tenderly alive to its own sufferings, but without the fortitude to bear them. He is, however, human in his distresses . . . The sufferings of the man make us forget that he ever was a king. . . .

A more affecting passage of the loneliness of a state of exile can hardly be given than by what Bolingbroke . . . observes of his having "sighed his English breath in foreign clouds"; or than that conveyed in Mowbray's complaint at being banished for life . . . How very beautiful is all this ["The language I have learned these forty years" etc.], and at the same time how very *English* too! . . . .

There is neither truth nor honour in all these noble persons [Fitzwater, Surrey, Aumerle, Percy]: they answer words with words, as they do blows with blows, in mere self-defence: nor have they any principle whatever but that of courage in maintaining any wrong they dare commit, or any falsehood which they find it useful to assert. . . .

The characters of old John of Gaunt and of his brother York, uncles to the King, the one stern and foreboding, the other honest, good-natured, doing all for the best, and therefore doing nothing, are well kept up. The speech of the former, in praise of England, is one of the most eloquent that ever was penned. . . .

The character of Bolingbroke . . . is drawn with a masterly hand:—patient for occasion, and then steadily availing himself of it, seeing his advantage afar off, but only seizing on it when he has it within reach, humble, crafty, bold, and aspiring, encroaching by regular but slow degrees, building power on opinion, and cementing opinion by power . . . His bold assertion of his own rights, his pretended submission to the king, and the ascendancy which he tacitly assumes over him in his power, are characteristic traits of this ambitious and political usurper. But the part of Richard himself gives the chief interest to the play. His folly, his vices, his misfortunes, his reluctance to part with the crown, his fear to keep it, his weak and womanish regrets, his starting tears, his fits of hectic passion, his smothered majesty, pass in succession before us, and make a picture as natural as it is affecting.

Walter Pater, "Shakespeare's English Kings," in *Appreciations* (1894).

With a prescience of the Wars of the Roses, of which his errors were the original cause, it is Richard who best exposes Shakespeare's own constant sentiment concerning war, and especially that sort of civil war which was then recent in English memories. The soul of Shakespeare, certainly, was not wanting in a sense of the magnanimity of warriors. The grandiose aspects of war, its magnificent apparelling, he records monumentally enough —the "dressing of the lists," the lion's heart, its unfaltering haste thither in all the freshness of youth and morning . . . Only, with Shakespeare, the afterthought is immediate:—"They come like sacrifices in their trim." . . . This sentiment Richard reiterates very plaintively, in association with the delicate sweetness of the English fields, still sweet and fresh, like London and her other fair towns in that England of Chaucer, for whose soil the exiled Bolingbroke is made to long so dangerously, while Richard on his return from Ireland salutes it—"That pale, that white-fac'd shore,—/ As a long-parted mother with her child . . ." Then (of Bolingbroke) "Ere the crown he looks for live in peace,/Ten thousand bloody crowns of mothers' sons/Shall ill become the flower of England's face . . ."—asks York, "So many miles upon her peaceful bosom/ Frighting her pale-fac'd visages with war?" . . . bruising "Her/ flowerets with the armed hoofs/Of hostile paces." Perhaps it is not too fanciful to note in this play a peculiar recoil from the mere instruments of warfare, the contact of the "rude ribs," the "flint bosom," of Barkloughly Castle or Pomfret . . . It is as if the lax, soft beauty of the king took effect, at least by contrast, on everything beside.

One gracious prerogative, certainly, Shakespeare's English kings possess: they are a very eloquent company, and Richard is the most sweet-tongued of them all. In no other play perhaps is there such a flush of those gay, fresh, variegated flowers of speech—colour and figure, not lightly attached to, but fused into, the very phrase itself —which Shakespeare cannot help dispensing to his characters, as in this "play of the Deposing of King Richard the Second," an exquisite poet if he is nothing else, from first to last, in light and gloom alike, able to see all things poetically, to give a poetic turn to his conduct of them, and refreshing with his golden language the tritest aspects of that ironic contrast between the pretensions of a king and the actual necessities of his destiny. What a garden of words! With him, blank verse, infinitely graceful, deliberate, musical in inflexion, becomes indeed a true "verse royal," that rhyming lapse, which to the Shakespearian ear, at least in youth, came as the last touch of refinement on it, being here doubly appropriate. His eloquence blends with that fatal beauty, of which he was so frankly aware, so amiable to his friends, to his wife, of the effects of which on the people his enemies were so much afraid, on which Shakespeare himself dwells so attentively as the "royal blood" comes and goes in the face with his rapid changes of temper. As happens with sensitive natures, it attunes him to a congruous suavity of manners, by which anger itself becomes flattering: it blends with his merely youthful hopefulness and high spirits, his sympathetic love for gay people, things, apparel—"his cote of gold and stone, valued at thirty thousand marks," the novel Italian fashions he preferred, as also with those real amiabilities that made people forget the darker touches of his character, but never tire of the pathetic reversal of his fall, the meekness of which would have seemed merely abject in a less graceful performer. . . .

Strangely enough, Shakespeare supposes him an over-confident believer in that divine right of kings, of which people in Shakespeare's time were coming to hear so much. . . .

Shakespeare's kings are not, nor are meant to be, great men: rather, little or quite ordinary humanity, thrust upon greatness, with those pathetic results, the natural self-pity of the weak heightened in them into irresistible appeal to others as the net result of their royal prerogative. One after another, they seem to lie composed in Shakespeare's embalming pages, with just that touch of nature about them, making the whole world akin, which has infused into their tombs at Westminster a rare poetic grace.

Edward Dowden, *Shakspere* (1899).

Having in *Richard III* . . . brought the civil wars of England to an issue and an end, Shakspere turned back to the reign of the earlier Richard, whose deposition led the way to the disputed succession and the conflicts of half a century later. The interest of the play centres in two connected things—the personal contrast between the falling and the rising kings, and the political action of each; the misgovernment of the one inviting and almost justifying the usurpation of the other. At the outset, Shakspere fixes the attention upon the murder of the King's uncle, the Duke of Gloucester, who was said by Mowbray to have died in his custody at Calais, but who was not unreasonably believed to have been put to death by Richard's order. Bolingbroke in striking at Mowbray was striking at Richard, and a dark deed of violence is brought into notice as the starting-point of the events which led to Richard's fall. But he has not only done violence to one of his own house, he has wronged the people of England. His upstart favourites, his blank charters, his farming of the realm, are so many blows pointed at the life of his country, and, as has been observed, the national aspect of the quarrel is brought forward by Hereford's proud assertion of his nationality, and by Gaunt's magnificent eulogy of England. But Shakspere—although no zealot in behalf of the divine right of kings —does not applaud usurpation as the means of destroying a tyranny;

from the Bishop of Carlisle's lips proceeds a prophecy of the future horrors of civil war which must ensue from the violent dethronement of the king . . .

Bolingbroke . . . is a man framed for such material success as waits on personal ambition. He is not, like his son Henry V., filled with high enthusiasm and sacred force derived from the powers of heaven and of earth. All Bolingbroke's strength and craft are his own. His is a resolute gaze which sees his object far off, and he has persistency and energy of will to carry him forward without faltering. He is not cruel, but shrinks from no deed that is needful to his purpose because the deed is cruel. His faculties are strong and well-knit. There is no finer contrast in Shakspere's historical plays than that between the figures of the formidable king of deeds, and the romantic king of hectic feelings and brilliant words.

William Butler Yeats, "At Stratford on Avon," in *Ideas of Good and Evil* (1903).

I cannot believe that Shakespeare looked on his Richard II with any but sympathetic eyes, understanding indeed how ill-fitted he was to be King, at a certain moment of history, but understanding that he was lovable and full of capricious fancy . . . To suppose that Shakespeare preferred the men who deposed his King is to suppose that Shakespeare judged men with the eyes of a Municipal Councillor weighing the merits of a Town Clerk.

A. C. Bradley, *Shakespearean Tragedy* (1905).

When he [a prince] falls suddenly from the height of earthly greatness to the dust, his fall produces a sense of contrast, of the powerlessness of man, and of the omnipotence—perhaps the caprice —of Fortune or Fate, which no tale of private life can possibly rival.

Such feeling are constantly evoked by Shakespeare's tragedies, —again in varying degrees. Perhaps they are the very strongest of the emotions awakened by the early tragedy of *Richard II.*, where they receive a concentrated expression in Richard's famous speech about the antic Death, who sits in the hollow crown "That rounds the mortal temples of a king," grinning at his pomp, watching till his vanity and his fancied security have wholly encased him round, and then coming and boring with a little pin through his castle wall.

Frederick S. Boas, *Shakspere and His Predecessors* (1910).

It is the natural mistake of a weak nature to think it is enough to banish a dangerous enemy without striking at the real source of his power, which lies in the wide-spread popular disaffection. A vivid glimpse into Richard's maladministration is given in his interview with the parasites, Bagot and Green, before he sets out for the Irish war. The realm is let out to farm; blank charters are issued for the levy of "benevolences"; the news of John of Gaunt's approaching death is hailed with delight as making his coffers, private property though they be, an easy prey . . . The moment the breath is out of the old hero's body [Richard's immediate purpose] is to seize "The plate, coin, revenue, and movables/Whereof our uncle Gaunt did stand possessed." Such a wanton invasion of the rights of inheritance is too much for even the pliant York—last left of Richard's uncles—who plucks up heart to point out that he is setting a suicidal precedent . . . But again Richard is deaf to good counsel, though with a singular lack of judgement he appoints this very York, unstable as water, and chagrined by his nephew's contempt for his warning words, to be governor of England during the Irish campaign. Thus, with a mere figurehead presiding over the realm, with the Commons alienated by oppressive imposts, and the nobles alarmed at the illegal outrage upon the rights of one of their order, England, during Richard's absence, lies at the mercy of a bold aspirant to the throne. With characteristic promptitude Bolingbroke seizes his opportunity . . . York, powerless to cope with such a crisis, virtually submits to the invader, whose ultimate claims are clear enough to him, by deciding to "remain as a neuter." But Bolingbroke preferring to keep so impartial a personage under his own eye, carries him in his train to Bristol, where he gives proof that his objects are not merely private by sending to their death Richard's favourites, Bushy and Green, or, in his own phrase, weeding the commonwealth of its "caterpillars." In executing such summary justice Bolingbroke is already exercising the functions of an uncrowned king . . .

While Richard's bearing earns the contempt of the practical statesman, it is not without a certain wistful charm that appeals especially to those of his nearer private circle. At intervals during the progress of the drama the Queen has been shown in the background, and her tender feeling for her "sweet" lord proves his

attractive power. As she sees him pass on the way to confinement,
. . . she weeps to see her "fair rose wither," though mingled with
her sorrow is an indignant feeling that "pupil-like" he takes his
correction mildly, and kisses the rod. But it is impossible to shame
Richard out of his luxury of grief into manly self-approach, and it
is with conceits and flourishes on his lips that he takes his last
farewell of his faithful bride. Faithful too is the poor groom who
visits him in prison . . .

Bolingbroke, though he has no personal malice against him,
feels his seat unsteady while Richard lives . . . The deed [Richard's
murder] arouses no unseemly exultation in Bolingbroke's breast; he
protests, and without hypocrisy: "My soul is full of woe/That blood
should sprinkle me to make me grow." He is already beginning to
feel the first strokes of Nemesis. An abortive conspiracy is formed
at Oxford for his overthrow, and he has to sentence his brother-in-
law to death for taking part in it. Nor is this his only domestic
trouble. He is cut to the heart by the riotous conduct of his "unthrifty son."

John Masefield, *William Shakespeare* (1910).

Treachery in some form is at the root of all Shakespearean
tragedy. In this play it takes many forms, among which two are
principal, the treachery of a king to his duty as a king, and the
treachery of a subject to his duty as a subject. As usual in Shakespearean tragedy, the play is filled full by the abundant mind of
the author with illustrations of his idea. The apricocks at Langley
are like King Richard, the sprays of the trees like Bolingbroke, the
weeds like the King's friends. Everybody in the play (even the horse
in the last act) is in passionate relation to the central idea.

King Richard is of a type very interesting to Shakespeare. He is
wilful, complex, passionate, with a beauty almost childish and a
love of pleasure that makes him greedy of all gay, light, glittering
things . . . He loves that kind of false, delicate beauty which is made
in societies where life is too easy. There is much that is beautiful in
him. He has all the charm of those whom the world calls the
worthless. His love is a woman, as beautiful and unreal as himself.
He fails because, like other rare things, he is not common . . . As a
king, Richard neglects his duties with that kind of wilfulness which
the world never fails to punish . . . He rebukes devotion to duty

by banishing Bolingbroke, who tries to rid him of a traitor. He rebukes old age and wisdom in the truly great person of old John of Gaunt. Worst, and most unkingly of all, he is uncapable of seeing and rewarding the large generosity of mind that makes sacrifices for an idea. Richard, who likes beautiful things, cannot see the beauty of old, rough, dying Gaunt, who condemns his own son to exile rather than bertay his idea of justice. Bolingbroke, who cares for nothing but justice. . . , is deeply and nobly generous to York, who would condemn his own son, and to the Bishop of Carlisle, who would die rather than not speak his mind. Men who sacrifice themselves are a king's only props. Richard allies himself with men who prefer to sacrifice the country.

It is a proof of the greatness of Shakespeare's vision, that Richard is presented to us both as the traitor and the betrayed . . . He is not fitted for kingship, but life has made him a king. Life, quite as much as temperament, is to blame for his tragedy. When life and temperament have thrust him from kingship, this wilful, passionate man, so greedy and heady in his hurry to be unjust, is unlike the monster that office made him. He is no monster then, but a man, not even a man like ourselves, but a man of singular delicacy of mind, sensitive, strangely winning, who wrings our hearts with pity by his sense of his tragedy . . . Part of his tragedy is due to his being too late. Had he landed from Ireland one day earlier he would have found a force of Welshmen ready to fight for him. At the end of the play he discovers, too late, that he is weary of patience. He strikes out like a man, when he has no longer a friend to strike with him. He is killed by a man who finds, too late, that the murder was not Bolingbroke's intention . . .

Those scenes in the last acts which display the mind of the deposed king are all exquisite, though their beauty is not obvious to the many. There is a kind of intensity of the soul, so intense that it is obscure to the many till it is interpreted. Writers of plays know well how tamely words intensely felt may read. They know, too, how like fire upon many souls those words will be when the voice and the action give them their interpretation. *Richard II*, like other plays of spiritual tragedy, needs interpretation. When he wrote it, Shakespeare had not wholly the power that afterwards he achieved, of himself interpreting his vision by many-coloured images. It is not one of the beloved plays.

Hardin Craig, *Richard II* (1912).

There are two styles in the blank verse of *Richard II,* a plain style and a rhetorical style; and the two are used to offset each other. Richard, Gaunt, Mowbray, and the Queen almost speak on the higher level; and other characters, when they are under stress of great emotion . . . occasionally rise to a level of declamation. Bolingbroke, Northumberland, and others of their part are made to speak more directly and simply, with the manifest purpose of contrasting them as practical men with the more sentimental and less practical Gaunt, Richard and Richard's party. . . . In the speeches of the King himself . . . the normal level of prosaic life is marked off by his lapses into the plain style.

George Saintsbury, *Shakespeare* (1934)

The curious immature splendor of the conception of the title part is like nothing else in Shakespeare. The parallel with, and the suggestion given by, Marlowe's *Edward II* are, of course, unmistakable. But where Marlowe has given three Edwards, not perhaps irreconcilable with each other but not actually reconciled, Shakespeare's Richard *sibi constat* throughout, in weakness as in strength —he is sincere in his insincerity. Still, the part is not well supported . . . The chronicle sequence, encroaching rather on dramatic construction, is also noticeable; as is the fact . . . that there is practically no comic element whatever . . . [The beauty of the poetry is] of the "purple patch" or "fringe" kind and, it would seem, purposely so.

Mark Van Doren, *Shakespeare* (1934).

He [Shakespeare] has not made a great man of him [Richard]. He has made a poet, a great minor poet. The author of *Richard II* is perhaps more interested in poetry than he will ever be again . . . The particular power he is now discovering is . . . the power to write the English language musically—with a continuous melody and with unfailing reserves of harmony . . . Richard drops his pretense of being a major poet simultaneously with the surrender of his power, with the crumpling of his front. The break is sudden and . . . brilliant.

Hazelton Spencer, *The Art and Life of William Shakespeare* (1940).

The grave beauty of this play sets it apart from all the other histories . . . Except in the monologues of the stricken hero, the verse is seldom distinguished. It is not pedestrian; but its elevation is secured, not by the development in flashing metaphor of an idea, but by labored accumulation of too obviously "poetic" diction . . . The play as a whole falls between the two stools of tragedy and chronicle-history.

E. M. W. Tillyard, *Shakespeare's History Plays* (1946).

Richard II lacks the sustained vitality of *Richard III,* being less interesting and less exacting in structure and containing a good deal of verse which by the best Shakespearean standards can only be called indifferent. . . .

Of all Shakespeare's plays *Richard II* is the most formal and ceremonial . . . The very actions tend to be symbolic rather than real . . . There is an elaboration and a formality in the cosmic references, scarcely to be matched in Shakespeare.

Ivor Brown, *Shakespeare* (1949).

[On the last scene of the play.] This is Pantomime poetry. The only conclusion I can draw is that Shakespeare has been using an older play on this theme lying in the possession of the Chamberlain's Men and that when he had seen his King "Spur-galled and tired by jauncing Bolingbroke" . . . and left him murdered in Pomfret Castle by Sir Pierce of Exton, he could not be bothered to rewrite the clearing-up lines and left them as they stood.

Leonard F. Dean, *"Richard II:* The State and the Image of the Theatre" (1952).

The ordeal by combat was a social institution, like the courtroom process which developed from it, that was deliberately designed to impose a stereotyped or unnatural character upon the participants. The real feelings of Richard, Bolingbroke, Mowbray, and even Gaunt are necessarily masked to a large extent by the calculated neutrality of the ceremony. We sense at once that the king and the nobles are reading lines, that their social behavior is

play-acting. Our subsequent judgment that the ceremony is a hypo-
critical disguise, that it will not cure the disorder which it is
momentarily suppressing, is the product both of the glib ritualistic
style and of those few lines in which contrary emotions come to
the surface.

Peter Ure, *King Richard II* (1956).

The play is in four unequal phases:

(i) Richard as king; the political crises with which he is
   faced . . . , and his lack of wisdom in dealing with them.
   [I/i-II/i/223]
(ii) Bolingbroke's invasion, and the transference of real power.
   [II/1/224-III/i]
(iii) Richard's deposition . . . [III/ii-V/i]
(iv) Bolingbroke as king; his mastery in a political crisis. [V/ii-
   end]

. . . [Shakespeare] placed the emphasis on Richard's nature and
behaviour, and gave his play the order and unity of biography.

G. B. Harrison, *Shakespeare at Work: 1592-1603* (1958).

None of the characters in this story came near his [Shake-
speare's] own experience, and he reverted to the earlier poetizing
method, indulging himself in fine writing and an enjoyment of
phrase making; so that Richard was a sonneteer's king, a creature
of exquisite sentimentality. He [combined, like Christopher Mar-
lowe] a cynical disregard for ordinary morality with an intense
beauty of fancy. Shakespeare revelled in the mere poetry of the
speeches; but at the same time he did not forget that fine writing by
itself would never make a play.

Una Ellis-Fermor, *Shakespeare the Dramatist* (1961).

The thought of Bolingbroke in certain scenes [II, iii and IV, i]
. . . is potentially revealed to us even in those passages where he is
silent and other men are speaking . . . And we can, if we wish, make
each of these other men in turn the centre of our attention and
then, when they in turn are silent, their thought will similarly be

revealed to us while others speak. It is not merely a matter of Shakespeare's identifying himself with each in turn, with each man as he comes to life in speech, but with each man's momentarily hidden life for so long as he is within the framework of the play, and, if necessary, beyond it.

H. M. V. Matthews, *Character and Symbol in Shakespeare's Plays* (1962).

We never see in existence the ordered Kingdom ruled with justice and mercy in accord with the purposes of God. The chorus-like figures of the gardeners . . . make the comparison of state and garden in a style as formal as that of the Elizabethan knot and herb gardens which they praise [*Cut off the heads of too fast growing sprays,* etc., III, iv, 34-47]. Richard himself does not conform to the pattern; that is both his sin and his tragedy, and the divine purpose is once again thwarted.

C. B. Purdom, *What Happens in Shakespeare* (1963).

This king is by no means wholly admirable, for he appears to be homosexual, causing him to be unbalanced and wayward, with the result that he wastes his kingdom, and his behaviour calls for rebellion. This grave fault is not disguised in the play, but is set in the light of the king's own eyes not as others saw it. Looked at objectively, another story could be told, but we are invited to view it as does the hero himself . . . Gaunt's death-episode is Richard's judgement on himself, otherwise it is difficult to explain; for why give Gaunt the first good speech in the play, unless the thoughts are Richard's?

A. L. Rowse, *William Shakespeare* (1964).

[The deposing of Richard] was a sin, it struck away the constitutional basis of government in England, it left the road wide open for the naked conflicts of power, into which public life consequently degenerated. It released a stream of blood, as Richard prophesied: "The blood of English shall manure the ground . . ." This was no very inaccurate description of the War of the Roses, to which Richard's deposition ultimately gave rise.

Oscar James Campbell and **Edward G. Quinn,** "Richard II," in
The Reader's Encyclopedia of Shakespeare (1966).

Richard II is a self-conscious poet, whose speeches and attitudes
are those of an actor playing the parts that Fate has assigned him.
. . . [He] is a self-absorbed lyric poet reciting lines that he invents
extempore. . . . Richard undoes himself. . . . [His] appeals for
sympathy are thus neutralized by his exaggerated sensibility toward
himself and his exaggerated apathy toward the concerns of everyone
else.

Suggestions for Further Reading

Albright, E. M., "Shakespeare's *Richard II* and the Essex Conspiracy," in *Publications of the Modern Language Association,* 1927, pp. 686-720.

Armstrong, W. A., "The Elizabethan Conception of the Tyrant," in *Review of English Studies,* July 1946.

Boas, F. S., *Shakspere and His Predecessors* (John Murray, 1910).

Bogard, T., "Shakespeare's Second Richard," in *Publications of the Modern Language Association,* 1955, pp. 192-204.

Bonnard, G. A., "The Actor in *Richard II,*" in *Shakespeare-Jahrbuch,* 1952, pp. 87-101.

Bradbrook, W. G., *Shakespeare and Elizabethan Poetry* (Chatto & Windus, 1951).

Brown, I., *Shakespeare* (Collins, 1949).

Campbell, L. B., *Shakespeare's Histories* (San Marino, Huntington Library, 1947).

Campbell, O. J. & Quinn, E. G., *The Reader's Encyclopedia of Shakespeare* (Thos. Y. Crowell, 1966).

Charlton, H. B., "Shakespeare, Politics and Politicians" (English Association Pamphlet, Number 72, 1929).

Coleridge, S. T., *Shakespearean Criticism* (Dutton, 1960).

Courtenay, T. P., *Commentaries on the Historical Plays of Shakespeare* (H. Colburn, 1840).

Davy, S., "The Relation of Poetry to History," in *Transactions of the Royal Society,* 2d Series, 1903.

Dean, L. F., "*Richard II*: The State and Image of the Theatre," in *Publications of the Modern Language Association,* 1952, pp. 211-18.

Doran, M., "Imagery in *Richard II* and in *Henry IV,*" in *Modern Language Review,* 1942, pp. 113-22.

Ellis-Fermor, U., *Shakespeare the Dramatist* (Methuen, 1961).

Harrison, G. B., *Shakespeare at Work: 1592-1603* (Ann Arbor Paperbacks, 1958).

Hazlitt, W., *Characters of Shakespeare's Plays* (Dutton, 1906).

Hearnshaw, F. J. C., "Shakespeare as Historian," in *The Contemporary Review*, 1923, pp. 729-38.

Lee, Sir S. & Chambers, Sir E. K., *A Shakespeare Reference Library* (English Association Pamphlet, Number 61, 1925).

MacManaway, J. G., "Richard II at Covent Garden," in *Shakespeare Quarterly*, 1964, pp. 161-75.

Marriott, J. A. K., *English History in Shakespeare* (Macmillan Co., 1946).

Masefield, J., *Shakespeare* (Butterworth, 1911).

O'Connell, R. L., "A Stage History of *Richard II*," in *Listener*, 1954, p. 225.

Pater, Walter, *Appreciations* (Macmillan Co., 1894).

Provost, F., "The Sorrows of Shakespeare's Richard II," in *Studies in English Renaissance Literature* (edited by W. F. McNeir) (Baton Rouge, 1962).

Ribner, I., "Bolingbroke, a True Macchiavelian," in *Modern Language Quarterly*, 1948, pp. 117-84.

Saintsbury, G., *Shakespeare* (Macmillan Co., 1934).

Schelling, F. E., *The English Chronicle Play* (Macmillan Co., 1902).

Scott-Giles, C. W., *Shakespeare's Heraldry* (Dent, 1950).

Spencer, H., *The Art and Life of William Shakespeare* (Harcourt, Brace, 1940).

Stirling, B., "Bolingbroke's 'Decision,' " in *Shakespeare Quarterly*, 1951, pp. 27-34.

Tillotson, K., "Drayton and *Richard II*: 1597-1600," in *Review of English Studies*, 1939, pp. 172-9.

Tillyard, E. M. W., *Shakespeare's History Plays* (Macmillan Co., 1946).

Van Doren, M., *Shakespeare* (Holt, 1939).

Warner, B. E., *English History in Shakespeare* (Longman's Green, 1894).

Wilkinson, B., "The Deposition of Richard II and Accession of Henry IV," in *English Historical Review*, 1939, pp. 215-39.

Wilson, J. D., "The Political Background of *Richard II* and *Henry IV*," in *Shakespeare-Jahrbuch*, 1939, pp. 36-51.

NOTES

NOTES

NOTES

NOTES

NOTES

NOTES

NOTES